Diving & Snorkeling

Red Sea

Jean-Bernard Carillet

Gavin Anderson

Pete Harrison

LONELY PLANET PUBLICATIONS
Melbourne • Oakland • London • Paris

Diving & Snorkeling Red Sea
- A Lonely Planet Pisces Book

2nd Edition – May 2001
1st Edition – 1995 Gulf Publishing Company

Published by
Lonely Planet Publications
90 Maribyrnong St., Footscray, Victoria 3011, Australia

Other offices
150 Linden Street, Oakland, California 94607, USA
10a Spring Place, London NW5 3BH, UK
1 rue du Dahomey, 75011 Paris, France

Photographs
by photographers as indicated

Front cover photograph, by Gavin Anderson
The stern of the *Salem Express*, Safaga Bay, Egypt

Back cover photographs
A man and his camel at the Pyramids of Giza, Egypt,
    by Jean-Bernard Carillet
Spanish dancer nudibranch at night, by Gavin Anderson
Life abounds on the Red Sea reefs, by Mark Webster

Most of the images in this guide are available for
    licensing from **Lonely Planet Images**
email: lpi@lonelyplanet.com.au

ISBN 1 86450 205 3

text & maps © Lonely Planet 2001
illustrations © Pete Harrison
photographs © photographers as indicated 2001
dive site maps are Transverse Mercator projection

LONELY PLANET and the Lonely Planet logo are
trademarks of Lonely Planet Publications Pty Ltd.

Printed by HingYip Printing Ltd., China

Contents

Authors

Jean-Bernard Carillet

After earning a degree in translation and international relations from La
Sorbonne Nouvelle in Paris, Jean-Bernard joined Lonely Planet's French office
before becoming a full-time author. A diving instructor and incorrigible trav-
eler, he has contributed to numerous Lonely Planet travel guides, including *Marseille, Corsica, South Pacific,*
Diving & Snorkeling Tahiti & French Polynesia and *Martinique, Dominique et Sainte-Lucie.*

Gavin Anderson

Gavin learned to dive in 1987 in Scotland, where he lives and works as a professional photographer and freelance writer. An accomplished underwater
photographer, he has written and taken photos for numerous UK dive and
travel magazines, as well as dive-travel brochures. Gavin has traveled and
dived worldwide. His first of many trips to the Red Sea was in 1988.

Pete Harrison

Pete is a professional journalist specializing in maritime industries and issues
for a number of publications and news services, including *The Times* and
Reuters. He has also written numerous articles and books on Red Sea diving
and fish life, largely based on four years' experience as a dive instructor on Red
Sea live-aboards. Pete has a degree in marine biology.

From the Authors

The authors would like to thank the following divers and friends whose invaluable assistance made this book
possible: In Eilat: Oren and Sam at Red Sea Sports Club. In Aqaba: Osama Rashty and Steve Rattle at
Aquamarina Diving Center. In Nuweiba: Pete and Yolanda at Emperor Divers. In Dahab: Rob Taylor and the
staff at Nesima Dive Center. In Sharm el-Sheikh: Woolfgang May at Sinai Dive Club; the crew at Sharks Bay,
especially Abu Sneda. In El Gouna: Joris Nieuwkoop at TGI; Nathalie, Adam, Huub and Tjoeke at Dive Tribe.
In Hurghada: Nigel Jarvis, manager of Easy Divers, his partner, Bob, and the staff, including Yasser, Hariba,
Mohammed, Caroline, Murielle, Wilma, Fathi and Keith; Ahmed and Fanny at UCPA; Morgan Meinecke at
Emperor Divers, who paved the way to Nuweiba; the staff at HEPCA and the Red Sea Protectorate. In Quseir:
Astrid Gburek, Anita Rhiner and the crew at Subex. In Marsa Alam: Hosam Helmy at Red Sea Diving Safari.
Also thanks to Brian Evans aboard the *Rosetta* and Pia Gottschalch and Ahmed Ali Abdlatif aboard the *Lady*
M. Special thanks to Colin Knight for writing the Saudi Arabia chapter and providing a resident's knowledge
of that country's unspoiled reefs.

Jean-Bernard Carillet would especially like to thank Kathleen Gray, for bringing native insights to his
dive site descriptions, and "my two partners in crime, Gavin and Pete, who survived my numerous emails,
phone calls, queries and demands in the frame of my coordinating job."

Gavin Anderson would especially like to thank his wife, Eileen, for her support and the following friends
for their help: David Easton, David and Sarah Hillel, Tony Backhurst, Neil Ploughman and Phil Conner.

Pete Harrison would like to thank Morgan and Jo, Martin and Jo, Johnny, Lisa, Ian, Duncan and T-money.

Photography Notes

Underwater, Gavin Anderson uses a variety of cameras and formats. For macro and close-up photography he
uses a Nikon N90s with a Nikkor 60mm lens in an Aquatica housing. For wide-angle photography he prefers
to use a Nikonos V with SB-105 strobes and either a 12mm Sea & Sea lens or a Nikonos 15mm lens. Topside,
Gavin works with the N90x and a variety of lenses. Topside, Jean-Bernard Carillet uses a Canon EOS-1 and
EOS-3 with a wide range of lenses. Gavin and Jean-Bernard use Fujichrome Velvia, Sensia and Provia slide
film and Kodachrome 100VS slide film.

Contributing Photographers

Gavin Anderson and Jean-Bernard Carillet took most of the photographs in this book. Thanks also to Colin
Knight, Edward Snijders, Mark Webster, Gavin Parsons, Mark Strickland, Lawson Wood and Thomas Hartwell
for their photo contributions.

From the Publisher

This second edition was published in Lonely Planet's U.S. office under the guidance of Roslyn Bullas, the Pisces Books publishing manager. David Lauterborn edited the text and photos with buddy checks from Wendy Smith, Roslyn Bullas and Suki Gear. Emily Douglas designed the cover and book. Justin Marler jazzed up the wreck illustrations. Navigating the nautical charts was cartographer John Spelman, who created the maps, with assistance from Colin Bishop, Sara Nelson and Annette Olson. U.S. cartography manager Alex Guilbert supervised map production. Lindsay Brown reviewed the Marine Life section for scientific accuracy. Portions of the text were adapted from Lonely Planet's *Middle East*, *Egypt* and *Israel & the Palestinian Territories*.

Pisces Pre-Dive Safety Guidelines

Before embarking on a scuba diving, skin diving or snorkeling trip, carefully consider the following to help ensure a safe and enjoyable experience:

- Possess a current diving certification card from a recognized scuba diving instructional agency (if scuba diving)
- Be sure you are healthy and feel comfortable diving
- Obtain reliable information about physical and environmental conditions at the dive site (e.g., from a reputable local dive operation)
- Be aware of local laws, regulations and etiquette about marine life and environment
- Dive at sites within your experience level; if possible, engage the services of a competent, professionally trained dive instructor or divemaster

Underwater conditions vary significantly from one region, or even site, to another. Seasonal changes can significantly alter site and dive conditions. These differences influence the way divers dress for a dive and what diving techniques they use.

There are special requirements for diving in any area, regardless of location. Before your dive, ask about environmental characteristics that can affect your diving and how trained local divers deal with these considerations.

Warning & Request

Things change—dive site conditions, regulations, topside information. Nothing stays the same for long. Your feedback on this book will be used to help update and improve the next edition. Excerpts from your correspondence may appear in *Planet Talk*, our quarterly newsletter, or *Comet*, our monthly email newsletter. Please let us know if you do not want your letter published or your name acknowledged.

Correspondence can be addressed to:
Lonely Planet Publications
Pisces Books
150 Linden Street
Oakland, CA 94607
email: pisces@lonelyplanet.com

Introduction

The Red Sea boasts a legendary reputation among divers. In only a few decades it has become a mecca for scuba enthusiasts from around the world, who come to experience its vibrant marine life, other-worldly wrecks and magnificent reef formations.

MARK WEBSTER

Color, more than anything else, defines its reefs. Golden shoals of anthias, shimmering silversides, great swaths of purple soft corals and clouds of royal-blue fusiliers are all set against the backdrop of a deep-blue abyss streaked with shafts of sunlight.

Rich hues in the sea are matched by a wealth of culture on land—the heritage of eight countries and five millennia of civilization. Egypt flaunts its own national treasures—the pyramids, the Valley of the Kings—but there are equal wonders elsewhere. The architecture of Yemen, for example, is absolutely stunning. And several thousand years before tipsy tourists wandered the streets in search of their hotels, a handful of biblical refugees wandered the wilderness in Sinai.

Despite a burgeoning economy, however, Egypt is hardly the empire-builder it once was. This is dangerous philosophical territory and somewhat of a chip on the

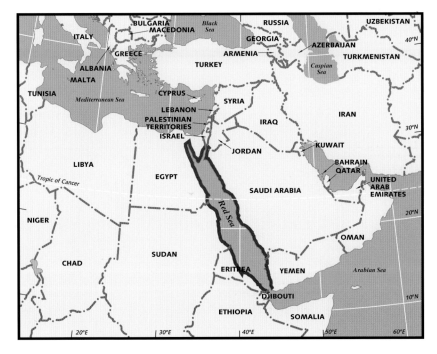

national shoulder. But the fact is that Egypt, and the region as a whole, offers something better than monuments to dead kings—a culture of hospitality. Through turbulent changes the region has never lost sight of life's raison d'être: spending leisurely hours with family and friends.

In the end, diving in the Red Sea is about more than just blowing bubbles. It's about coming back up to laugh and chat with fellow divers while you drink tea and watch the setting sun turn the sea red.

This book describes 108 sites throughout the Red Sea, including dives in **Israel**, **Jordan** and **Saudi Arabia**, the Egyptian regions of **Nuweiba & Dahab (North Sinai)**, **Sharm el-Sheikh (South Sinai)**, **El Gouna & Hurghada**, **Safaga**, **Quseir** and the **Deep South**, as well as the countries of the **Southern Red Sea**. You'll find detailed site information, including topography, depth range, typical marine life and recommended diver expertise. Detailed sketches accompany several wreck descriptions, and the Marine Life section offers a peek at the Red Sea's most common vertebrates and invertebrates.

While not intended to be a comprehensive travel guide, the book also offers practical topside information, as well as summaries of the region's geography, history, activities and attractions.

JEAN-BERNARD CARILLET

Spend your time ashore exploring the region's eight countries or simply relaxing after a dive.

Overview

JEAN-BERNARD CARILLET

The Red Sea is a long, deep basin of water separating Africa and the Arabian Peninsula. It is nearly 2,000km (1,240 miles) long, but only 300km (185 miles) broad at its widest point and a mere 30km (19 miles) wide at its southernmost point, the Bab el-Mandeb Strait. In a word, this narrow strip of sea is almost enclosed.

Eight countries border its coastline. Egypt and Saudi Arabia split the lion's share, while Israel, Jordan, Sudan, Eritrea, Yemen and Djibouti also border the sea. Egypt, Israel and Jordan are the region's most popular destinations and attract millions of tourists annually.

Though it's a large and diverse region, cultural similarities are evident. One common denominator is the importance of Islam—except, of course, in Israel. Something else these countries share is the very hot, dry climate. The Red Sea is an oasis of life in a largely barren area.

Geography

Africa and the Arabian Peninsula are slowly inching apart, leaving a flooded rip in the earth's surface between them. This is the Red Sea. The countries bordering this geologic cleft share similar geographic patterns—coastlines flanked by narrow, arid coastal plains backed by jagged mountain ranges.

The sea stretches northwest-southeast. At its northern end it divides into two gulfs: the Gulf of Aqaba, bordered by Egypt, Israel, Jordan and Saudi Arabia, and the Gulf of Suez, flanked by Egypt. The Sinai Peninsula separates the gulfs. The mountains of Sinai and Jordan line either side of the Gulf of Aqaba, mirrored underwater by jagged cliffs that tumble vertically to the seafloor more than 1,600m (5,250ft) below. In contrast, the Suez is quite shallow, about 63m (200ft) deep, and is bordered by coastal plains.

Farther down the Egyptian coast are the resorts of Hurghada and Safaga. The underwater topography here is typified by shallow inshore shelves, with easy,

Why the "Red" Sea?

There are two schools of thought on what inspired the name Red Sea. Some believe the sea was named after the red rock mountain ranges that surround it. Others insist it was named for periodic algae blooms that tinge the water a reddish-brown. Whatever the spark, it inspired ancient mariners to dub these waters *Mare Rostrum*—the Red Sea.

protected diving among myriad islands and reefs. Offshore these shelves drop away in dramatic walls, which in strong currents allow hard-core drift diving.

Southern Egypt follows a similar pattern. The renowned Fury Shoal and St. John's Reef provide sheltered sites, while the offshore islands—the Brothers, Daedalus, Zabargad and Rocky—tower up from the depths. On the opposite shore, the Saudi coast remains virtually unexplored.

Sudan marks the last of the blue-water drop-offs. South of here steep walls and coral reefs give way to boulder-strewn sandy slopes, with occasional coral outcrops. Sand and boulders may not sound exciting, but the stunning marine life and virgin sites more than compensate.

At its southern tip the Red Sea narrows again at Bab el-Mandeb Strait, where its waters mingle with those of the Gulf of Aden.

Much of the coast follows the same pattern—rugged ranges sloping into a deep blue sea.

History

The northern Red Sea is sandwiched between the Nile Valley and the Fertile Crescent of Mesopotamia, considered the birthplace of civilization. The Nile Valley was home to some of the earliest known organized societies, dating back to about 3100 BC. In the Bible, the Israelites were delivered from the Egyptian army by the celebrated parting of the Red Sea, and Sinai is the "great and terrible wilderness" they crossed in search of the Promised Land.

In the 2nd and 1st centuries BC, Roman legionnaires conquered much of the area, including Palestine (present-day Israel) and finally Egypt in 30 BC. Only the desert nomads and frankincense kingdoms of South Arabia remained independent.

The coming of Islam transformed the region. Following a divine revelation, the Arabian preacher Mohammed rose to become a successful religious, political and military leader, unifying the region's tribes and conquering his hometown of

Watch Your Step

Despite what local tour operators may tell you, some areas of Sinai still contain land mines left over from the wars with Israel. Wherever you go, stick to tracks and don't explore that pristine beach until you've checked that it's safe with locals.

Mecca. He died in 632, but his successors quickly spread the new religion into neighboring countries.

The Mamluks and Ottomans exchanged blows up through the 16th century, when Europeans began to express an interest in the Middle East. By the 19th century the French and British had traded possession of Egypt and progressively seized control of several countries. The Suez Canal opened in 1869, easing access to the Red Sea.

In the wake of WWI the French and British partitioned the Ottoman empire, the French taking control of Syria and Lebanon, while the British retained Egypt and acquired Palestine, Transjordan and Iraq.

The region next hit the headlines following WWII. In 1947 the UN voted to partition Palestine and allow Jewish immigration. The Arab side rejected the plan, while the Jews declared creation of the state of Israel. The first Arab-Israeli war was fought in 1948.

In 1967 the Egyptian army moved into Sinai and blockaded the Strait of Tiran, effectively closing the Israeli port of Eilat. Israel retaliated and in six days of fighting wrested control of Sinai from Arab forces. The next war, in 1973, ended in stalemate.

Egypt and Israel ended hostilities with the signing of the Camp David Accords in 1979. In 1994 Jordan became the second Arab country to sign a formal peace treaty with Israel. Traveling between these countries is now relatively easy and safe, and Sinai is no longer a battleground but a playground for divers from around the world.

Relics of war litter the region, including this submerged tank, now a spectacular wreck dive.

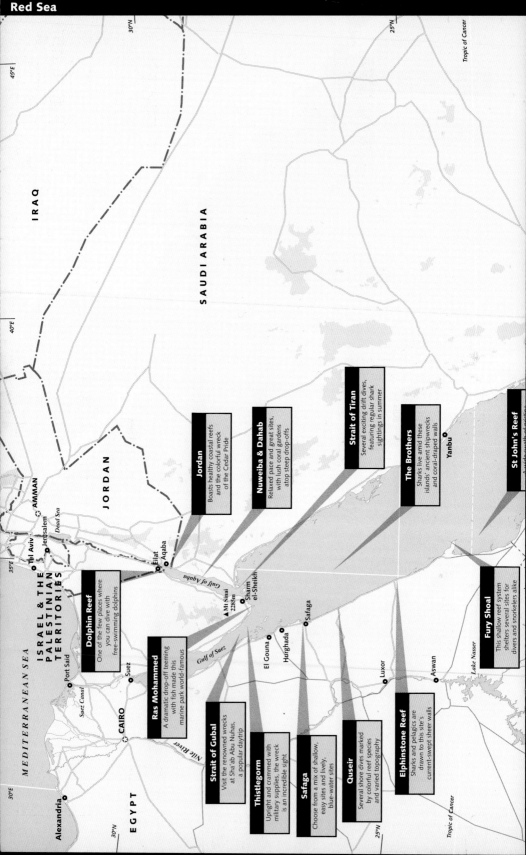

IRAQ

SAUDI ARABIA

JORDAN

ISRAEL & THE
PALESTINIAN
TERRITORIES

EGYPT

MEDITERRANEAN SEA

Tropic of Cancer

Suez Canal

Nile River

Gulf of Suez

Gulf of Aqaba

Dead Sea

Lake Nasser

▲ Mt Sinai
2285m

Alexandria

Port Said

AMMAN

Tel Aviv

Jerusalem

CAIRO

Suez

Eilat

Aqaba

Sharm
el-Sheikh

El Gouna

Hurghada

Safaga

Luxor

Aswan

Yanbu

Dolphin Reef
One of the few places where
you can dive with
free-swimming dolphins

Ras Mohammed
A dramatic drop-off teeming
with fish made this
marine park world-famous

Strait of Gubal
Visit the renowned wrecks
at Sha'ab Abu Nuhas,
a popular daytrip

Thistlegorm
Upright and crammed with
military supplies, the wreck
is an incredible sight

Safaga
Choose from a mix of shallow,
easy sites and lively,
blue-water sites

Queseir
Several shore dives marked
by colorful reef species
and varied topography

Elphinstone Reef
Sharks and pelagics are
drawn to this site's
current-swept sheer walls

Jordan
Boasts healthy coastal reefs
and the colorful wreck
of the Cedar Pride

Nuweiba & Dahab
Relaxed pace and great sites,
with lush coral gardens
atop steep drop-offs

Strait of Tiran
Several exciting drift dives,
featuring regular shark
sightings in summer

The Brothers
Sharks live amid these
islands' ancient shipwrecks
and coral-draped walls

St John's Reef
A wide

Fury Shoal
This shallow reef system
shelters several sites for
divers and snorkelers alike

30°E   35°E   40°E   45°E

30°N   25°N

Tropic of Cancer

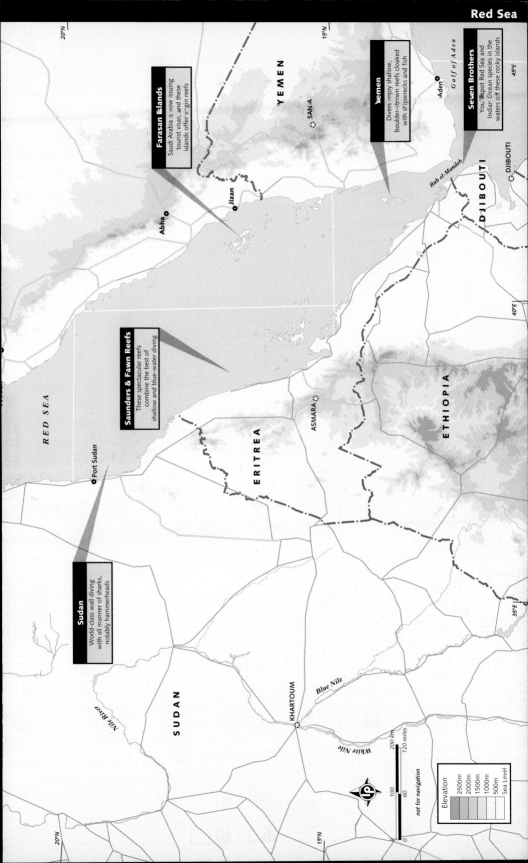

Farasan Islands
Saudi Arabia is now issuing tourist visas, and these islands offer virgin reefs

Yemen
Divers enjoy shallow, boulder-strewn reefs cloaked with shipwrecks and fish

Seven Brothers
You'll spot Red Sea and Indian Ocean species in the waters of these rocky islands

Saunders & Fawn Reefs
These spectacular reefs combine the best of shallow and blue-water diving

Sudan
World-class wall diving with all manner of sharks, notably hammerheads

RED SEA

Gulf of Aden

YEMEN

SAN'A

Aden

Abha

Jizan

Bab el-Mandeb

DJIBOUTI

DJIBOUTI

ERITREA

ASMARA

ETHIOPIA

Port Sudan

SUDAN

KHARTOUM

Blue Nile

White Nile

Nile River

20°N

15°N

15°N

20°N

45°E

40°E

35°E

Elevation
2500m
2000m
1500m
1000m
500m
Sea Level

200 km

120 miles

100

60

0

not for navigation

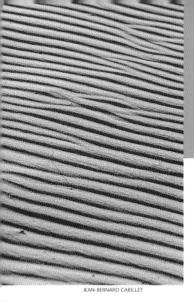
JEAN-BERNARD CARILLET

Practicalities

Climate

The regional climate is generally hot and dry, with strong prevailing winds that can affect dive conditions. Daytime temperatures vary depending on time and location, but they usually don't drop below 20°C (68°F) in winter (December to February) and consistently reach about 40°C (104°F) in summer (July and August).

The Red Sea itself is diveable year-round. Water temperatures vary from as low as 18°C (64°F) in the north in winter to almost 30°C (86°F) in the south in summer. Of course, within such a vast area there are notable variations.

Gulf of Aqaba

The gulf waters are gin-clear year-round. Desert winds from the north funnel down between the mountains of Sinai to the east and those of Jordan to the west. By the time they reach the Strait of Tiran, at the gulf's southern end, they often whip up large waves. Strong currents flow both north and south through the strait. If the current is running opposite the wind, the waves can reach a formidable size. Even as far north as Nuweiba and Dahab the waves can interfere with diving, especially since the sites there are shore dives.

At its northernmost end, the gulf's cooler waters attract many interesting species, including yellowmouth morays and Arabian smoke angelfish.

Gulf of Suez

As a rule of thumb, if the wind is blowing in the Gulf of Aqaba, then it is calm in the Suez. This has contributed to Sharm el-Sheikh's popularity among divers—as it straddles the point between the two gulfs, there are always good dive conditions on one side or the other. As in the Aqaba, the wind always blows from the north and strong currents flow both directions. Unlike the Aqaba, however, the Suez is shallow and sandy, and any wave action drastically limits visibility.

The water at this northern latitude is notably cool. Divers may want to wear semi-dry suits or even drysuits in the winter, when the water temperature dips to about 18°C (64°F).

Hurghada & Safaga

This region lies exposed to northerly winds, especially at Sha'ab Abu Nuhas. Many a live-aboard has sat inside its lagoon for days on end, waiting for a window of opportunity to visit the wrecks on the outer reef. Thankfully, myriad nearby islands offer alternatives for sheltered diving.

Wind-driven surface currents generally cancel out southerly currents, hence drift diving is typically done north to south. As the northern reef slopes are the most current-exposed, the corals and marine life along them are more profuse, particularly around Safaga. Water temperatures are a touch more forgiving than in the gulfs, though drysuits are still recommended in winter months.

The calm lagoon at Sha'ab Abu Nuhas offers refuge from wind-whipped waves.

Southern Egypt

South of Safaga the seas and weather remain predictable, with both wind and waves coming from the north. Currents also typically run north to south, reversing direction only during certain times of year. The waters from here to the Bab el-Mandeb Strait are warm year-round.

Southern Red Sea

Conditions south of Egypt are complex. First, the prevailing currents change, welling up from the south, a changeover that occurs off Sudan. Farther south still, off Yemen and Djibouti, the surface waves also come from the south. As a result, divers look to the southern reef slopes for the prime dive sites.

Language

Arabic is the official language of Jordan, Egypt, Saudi Arabia, Yemen and Sudan. It is also common in Eritrea. In Djibouti, French and Arabic are joint official languages. The national language of Israel is Hebrew.

English is widely understood and spoken in the region, and you'll have no trouble getting by. That said, it pays to learn a few words in Arabic and Hebrew. Any effort to speak with locals in their own language is well regarded.

Now You're Talking

	Egyptian Arabic	Hebrew
Hello	Salam alekum	Shalom
Goodbye	Maasalam	Lehitra'ot
Please	Min fadlak/fadlik	Bevakasha
Thank you	Shukran	Toda
How much?	Bikam?	Ah-desh hadah?
I don't understand	Ana mish fahem	Ani lo mevin(a)
yes	aywa	ken
no	la	lo
boat	markib	oniya
diving	rhats	tslila
water	maya	ma'im
fish	samak	dag

Suggested reading: Lonely Planet's *Egyptian Arabic phrasebook* and Lonely Planet's *Hebrew phrasebook*

EDWARD SNIJDERS

Getting There

Most visitors to the Red Sea arrive by air. Cairo (Egypt) is the largest international airport in the area and is directly linked to major cities in the U.S. (New York and Los Angeles), Australia and most countries in Western Europe. Amman (Jordan) and Tel Aviv (Israel) are also served by an excellent network of international airlines. In Israel, Jordan and Egypt, domestic air service is good, and you'll have no problem getting a connection to, respectively, Eilat, Aqaba and Sharm el-Sheikh or Hurghada. Saudi Arabia is also well connected to major cities in Europe and the U.S.

The southern Red Sea countries of Sudan, Yemen and Eritrea are best accessed through Cairo, using EgyptAir, the Egyptian national airline. Connections to Djibouti are made through Paris.

In addition to regular international flights, you'll find numerous charter flights at competitive prices, especially to Egypt. Most charter flights serve Sharm el-Sheikh and Hurghada. Consult a travel agent for the best deal.

Gateway Cities

Israel – Eilat

From its beginnings as a small desert outpost wedged between Egypt and Jordan, allowing Israel strategic access to the Red Sea, Eilat has transformed into a wanna-be beachfront Las Vegas. Glitzy ziggurat-hotels line a turquoise artificial lagoon, from which Disneyesque glass-bottomed boats set out on cruises around the bay. International hotels, shops and restaurants abound, and there are plenty of attractions for nondivers, both in the surrounding area and farther afield.

The airport is close to the town center. Some airlines fly direct to Eilat, while many charters connect via Ovda, an hour north. You can also fly into Tel Aviv and catch a connecting flight. Another option is to travel by bus or car from Jordan— but be prepared to be patient while crossing the border.

Dozens of luxury resorts line Eilat's preened, palm-fringed waterfront.

Jordan – Aqaba

Jordan's only coastal town, Aqaba has grown from a small pre-Roman fishing village into a major trading port and aquatic playground. Since the signing of the Camp David Accords, tourism has taken off (including the recent opening of several hotels). It's a relaxed place, with a good range of hotels and restaurants.

The airport is about 10km (6 miles) north of town. In the summer high season, airlines fly direct to Aqaba from several European cities; otherwise, visitors connect via Amman, Jordan's capital. You can also fly into Eilat and cross the Israeli border.

Standing atop the Giza Plateau for 46 centuries, the pyramids today are on the Cairo bus line.

Egypt – Cairo, Hurghada, Sharm el-Sheikh

Cairo is the usual gateway to the region, as it is served by flights from all directions. Though utterly congested and polluted, with one of the world's highest population densities, the city still captivates many visitors. In the space of a few hours it's possible to travel from the medieval backstreets of Islamic Cairo to the pharaonic majesty of the pyramids.

Once an isolated and modest fishing village, Hurghada is now a sprawling city, home to more than 35,000 people and 100-plus hotels and resorts that cater to sunseekers and divers from around the world. The city is the gateway to Egypt's southern dive sites, including Safaga, Quseir and Marsa Alam. Close to Hurghada's resort strip, the airport is well connected to Cairo and is also served by charter flights from several European cities. You'll have to leave town to find culture, perhaps joining a daytrip to the temples at Luxor. A budding resort town about 20km north of Hurghada, El Gouna is far quieter and more charming.

On the southeastern Sinai coast, Sharm el-Sheikh is a long-standing settlement initially developed by the Israelis. Greater Sharm el-Sheikh comprises two distinct areas: Sharm el-Sheikh city and the resort strip at Na'ama Bay, just 6km (4 miles) north. The two areas are rapidly blending together into one long development strip, with four- and five-star resorts geared to Europeans on package tours. Visitors can indulge in a variety of watersports, as well as day and overnight trips to Cairo. The airport is about 8km (5 miles) north of Na'ama Bay. You can fly direct from several European cities or via Cairo from other international destinations. A ferry from Hurghada runs twice weekly.

Getting Around

Several options exist for travel between countries in the Red Sea region, including by plane, bus, train, ferry boat or rental car. That said, border crossings range from inconvenient to dangerous to impossible. Saudi Arabia is still largely closed to visitors. Tourists traveling from Israel will have little trouble crossing into Jordan or Egypt, though they will not be welcomed into most other Middle Eastern and North African nations. Overland travel to countries of the southern Red Sea is unfeasible due to ongoing conflicts.

Is It Safe?

Tensions in the Middle East wax and wane. To get the latest regional travel advisories from the U.S. State Department, log on to their website at www.travel.state.gov/travel_warnings.html. Although the warnings are conservative and aimed primarily at Americans traveling abroad, the information is current and useful for travel-planning purposes.

Israel

Israel's small size and excellent road system combine to make bus travel the choice of public transport. Though less convenient and more limited, trains might be an option on certain routes. Shared taxis ply major intercity routes, hitting the road only when full. In cities you'll find regular taxis. Major car rental agencies have offices throughout Israel.

Jordan

Buses and minibuses link most major cities in Jordan, though service taxis are by far the most popular mode of transport. These run along set routes between most towns. Car rental is also an option, with many agencies in Amman and a few in Aqaba.

Egypt

Buses connect just about every city, town and village in Egypt. On major routes they boast comfortable seats and air conditioning. Train service is also an option, though the system is fairly outdated. Service taxis are one of the fastest ways to get around. They are generally big Peugeot 504 cars that run intercity routes. There are no set departure times—you just turn up and find a car. In resort towns you'll find microbuses or pickups. Several international car rental agencies have offices in Egypt.

Attitudes Toward Women

Middle Easterners are conservative, especially about matters concerning sex and women—local women, that is. Women are expected to be virgins when they marry, and a family's reputation can rest upon this point. The presence of foreign women presents, in the eyes of some Middle Eastern men, a way around these norms with ease and few consequences. Expect some verbal harassment and be on your guard for pinching or grabbing—though further advances are much less common.

Away from the beach resorts and big cities, Middle Easterners are also quite conservative about dress. Wearing shorts and a tight T-shirt on the street is, in some people's eyes, confirmation of the worst views held of Western women. Generally, the more skin you reveal, the more harassment you should expect. Take your cues from local dress codes.

EDWARD SNIJDERS

Entry

Israel

With few exceptions, a tourist visa is not required to visit Israel, just a passport, valid for at least six months from your date of entry. Exceptions include holders of passports from African and Central American countries, India, Singapore and some of the ex-Soviet republics. Tourists are normally allowed a three-month visit, although visitors entering through land borders with Egypt and Jordan are initially granted only a month's stay.

Those countries that refuse to recognize the Israeli state (Syria and the Gulf States, for example) also refuse to let anyone across their borders whose passport is marked by an Israeli stamp. If you plan to visit those countries, ask Israeli immigration officials to stamp only your entry permit and not your passport.

Jordan

Visas are required for all foreigners entering the country. These are issued at the border or airport on arrival or can be obtained from Jordanian consulates outside the country. Tourist visas are valid for stays of up to two weeks from the date of entry but are easily extended for up to three months.

Egypt

All foreigners entering Egypt, except nationals of Malta, South Africa, Zimbabwe and Arab countries, must obtain visas from Egyptian embassies or consulates overseas or at the airport upon arrival. A single-entry visa is valid for three months and entitles the holder to stay in Egypt for one month. Unless you plan to visit Ras Mohammed, it is more convenient (not to mention cheaper) to get a visa at Cairo airport, where the entire process takes only a few minutes.

Planning to Dive at Ras Mohammed?

You must obtain a full visa *before* arrival in Egypt in order to dive at Ras Mohammed National Park. The visa you obtain at the airport is a mini visa that lacks the applicable tax stamps, and Sinai entry permits are only valid between the Israeli border and Sharm el-Sheikh. There is no way to obtain the full visa while in Egypt. Live-aboard divers should check with their operators. Remember to bring your passport.

Other Countries

A visa is compulsory for all visitors to Sudan. The process is lengthy—up to two months—since applications are typically referred to Khartoum.

Except for citizens of Gulf Cooperation Council countries, everyone entering Yemen needs a visa, obtainable at any Yemeni consulate.

Except for French nationals, all visitors to Djibouti must apply for a visa. The visas are valid for one month.

Despite recent easing of travel restrictions, Saudi Arabia remains one of the hardest places in the world to visit. To obtain a tourist visa, you must have a Saudi sponsor.

Time

Israel, Jordan, Egypt, Sudan, Eritrea and Djibouti are two hours ahead of GMT. Saudi Arabia and Yemen are three hours ahead. When it is noon in Cairo, it is 11am in Paris, 10am in London, 5am in New York, 2am in San Francisco and 8pm in Sydney.

Money

In Israel the national currency is the new Israeli shekel, divided into 100 agorot. The currency in Jordan is the dinar, divided into 1,000 fils. In Egypt the unit of currency is the Egyptian pound, divided into 100 piastres. In Saudi Arabia the currency is the Saudi riyal, and in Yemen, the Yemeni riyal. In Sudan it is the new Sudanese dinar. Djibouti uses the Djibouti franc, while Eritrea still uses the Ethiopian birr, pending introduction of its own currency, the nafka.

In Israel, Jordan and Egypt, major credit cards are widely accepted at tourist establishments, including hotels, restaurants and dive centers. Changing money is also very easy in these countries, though most major currencies are accepted in cash or in traveler's checks. As for ATMs, they do exist but are not completely reliable, except in Israel.

Most divers visiting Sudan, Eritrea, Yemen and Djibouti go through a package tour aboard a live-aboard, thus avoiding the hassles of dealing with local currencies.

Electricity

The electric current in countries bordering the Red Sea is 220V AC, 50 Hz, with a round two-pin plug, except in Yemen, where a three-pin plug is used. You should bring your own adapter or converter, especially if you need to charge strobe batteries or dive lights.

Weights & Measures

All countries bordering the Red Sea use the metric system. In this book both metric and imperial measurements are given, except for specific references in dive site descriptions, which are given in metric units only. Please refer to the conversion chart provided on the inside back cover.

What to Bring

General

In Israel, Jordan and Egypt, there is very little you might need that you won't be able to find, though the choice may be more limited than at home. Sunglasses, sunscreen and a hat are essential. It's also a good idea to bring toiletries and prescription medicine.

It never gets cold in the region, so bring only lightweight clothing. Add a light sweater if you visit in winter, as it gets chilly at night. Also pack a windbreaker to keep you warm on the boat following a dive.

Visitors to Muslim countries, especially women, are strongly advised to dress conservatively and respect the local customs by not wearing swimsuits, shorts or other inappropriate clothing in town.

Dive-Related

Water temperatures can be surprisingly chilly in winter in the northern Red Sea, and it's a good idea to bring a 5 to 7mm wetsuit, especially if you plan repetitive dives or you're diving from a live-aboard. In the summer months a 3 to 5mm wetsuit is reasonable. In the southern Red Sea a 3mm suit will suffice year-round.

It's always best to bring your own dive gear. Though high-quality rental gear is available at most dive shops, it can be quite expensive. Most dive centers will check your C-card, so be sure to have it handy.

JEAN-BERNARD CARILLET

Never mind that this is the Middle East—you'll need a full wetsuit on most dives.

Underwater Photography

While film and processing services are readily available in Israel, Jordan and, to a lesser extent, Egypt, it is better to be self-sufficient. Bring your own film, batteries, converters and backup bodies and lenses. Rental equipment is available at some of the larger dive operations (check before departure). If you book a live-aboard trip, ask the operator whether the boat is equipped for film processing. Only the most luxurious ones are.

In Israel, Jordan and Egypt, cameras, video equipment and sometimes dive gear must be declared at customs. The serial numbers are often recorded in your passport to ensure you don't sell any of it. Israeli customs requires a refundable deposit on such equipment, while visitors to Egypt have reported being charged a hefty "import tax."

Business Hours

The day of rest throughout the region is Friday, except in Israel, where it is Saturday. Regarding actual business hours, there are no set rules. Shops have different hours at different times of the year, depending on the seasons. During Ramadan, the month-long fasting period for Muslims, most shops shut down in the afternoon.

Accommodations

Israel, Jordan and Egypt offer a wide range of accommodations, especially in the diving hubs, which are typically major resort towns. Places to stay range from

On the mainland, El Gouna's attractive resort strip is a playground for Egypt's privileged.

world-class hotels in the capitals and resort towns, to comfortable, mid-range hideaways, down to the most basic lodging houses and seaside camps.

Standards vary between countries, but price generally reflects amenities. Top-end hotels provide clean, air-conditioned, self-contained rooms with hot showers and toilets that work all the time. In the mid-range, rooms are self-contained, but there may not always be hot water, and there will probably be fans instead of air conditioning. Near the bottom end of the scale, hotel rooms are rather filthy.

Most resorts cater to divers and have an on-site dive shop. Many offer dive packages that include accommodations, half-board and airport transfers.

Live-aboards usually offer high-quality service and accommodations.

Dining & Food

Though the quality of food varies throughout the region, none of the countries covered in this book is famed for its local cuisine. Meat—usually lamb or chicken—bread, cabbage, rice and pastries comprise the basic staples. A pleasant feature is the availability of street food, nearly always cooked in front of you.

In the resort towns there is no shortage of Western-style restaurants, which range from burger bars to five-star buffets. Most hotels and resorts have an attached restaurant and serve decent international dishes.

Tea and coffee are consumed in copious quantities and are served strong, and juice stalls selling freshly squeezed fruit juices are common. While alcohol is forbidden in the eyes of many Muslims, it is freely available in larger cities and resorts, except in Saudi Arabia.

JEAN-BERNARD CARILLET

Restaurants range from seaside cafés to five-star buffets at the resorts.

Shopping

One of the travel highlights of Arabic countries is a visit to a *souq*, or market, where you can browse canvas-covered alleys past countless craft stands, clothing shops and fragrant spice stalls. The list of products varies by country but includes handicrafts, rugs and carpets, clothing, spices, jewelry, papyrus, *sheeshas* or *hookahs* (water pipes), brassware and copperware, leather goods and bottles of colored sand. Of course, there are also heaps of tacky souvenirs, from pyramid paperweights to belly-dancing outfits. In any case, bargaining is the rule, so come prepared.

Beware of vendors selling fake antiquities. In Egypt and Jordan it is illegal to export anything of antique value without a government permit.

How to Haggle Like a Pro

All prices are negotiable in the souq, and bargaining is expected. Prices of souvenirs are always inflated to allow for it. For those not used to it, bargaining can be a hassle, but keep your cool and remember it's a game, not a fight.

The first rule is never to show too much interest in the item you want to buy. Second, don't buy the first item that takes your fancy—take time to wander around.

Decide how much you would be happy paying and then express a casual interest in buying. The vendor will state their price, and you state a figure somewhat less than what you have fixed in your mind. So the bargaining begins. The shopkeeper will inevitably huff about how absurd your offer is and then tell you his "lowest" price. Still not low enough? Be insistent and keep smiling. If you still can't get your price, head toward the door. This often has the effect of closing the sale in your favor.

GAVIN ANDERSON

Activities & Attractions

GAVIN ANDERSON

From camel rides, dramatic landscapes and ancient tombs to felucca trips, buzzing souqs and labyrinthine medinas, this area of the world has much to offer. For centuries it has captured the imagination of countless adventurers and travelers. Visitors can still sleep beneath the stars on an overnight desert safari, unwind in a traditional Arabic teahouse and discover the mystical beauty of ancient mosques. Although staunchly conservative in some respects, this region is also among the most hospitable in the world.

The quality of tourist infrastructures varies widely by country. While Egypt, Israel, Jordan and Saudi Arabia offer visitors a spectrum of accommodations and restaurants and boast reliable services and public transportation, Sudan and Yemen still lack such resources, which hampers their tourism efforts.

Egypt

Birthplace of one of history's great civilizations, Egypt still reflects the glory of the pharaohs in the ancient monuments that dot the landscape. The unrivaled beauty of the Red Sea coast combines with natural and architectural marvels to make the country a fascinating destination.

Cairo, the nation's bustling capital city, boasts the nearby **Pyramids of Giza**, among the original Seven Wonders of the World. These spectacular edifices were pharaohs' tombs and repositories for all their worldly goods and treasures. The largest is the Great Pyramid of Cheops, which stands nearly 140m (460ft) high and was completed around 2600 BC. Follow up with a visit to the **Egyptian Museum**,

GAVIN ANDERSON

Bargain carefully for a camel ride at the pyramids.

GAVIN ANDERSON

King Tutankhamen holds court in the Egyptian Museum.

where more than 100,000 Egyptian antiquities and relics are on display. Also wander the lively, narrow alleyways of **Khan al-Khalili market**, where you can buy just about anything.

Down the Nile Valley, built on and around the 4,000-year-old site of ancient Thebes, **Luxor** will delight anyone with an interest in archaeology. It stands as one of the world's greatest open-air museums, with numerous temples, tombs and other archaeological splendors, including the **temples of Karnak** and **Valley of the Kings**. Daytrips from Hurghada and Quseir are regularly scheduled.

On the banks of Lake Nasser, close to the Sudanese border, don't miss the most photogenic of all Egypt's monuments, Ramses II's **Great Temple of Abu Simbel**, carved out of a mountainside between 1290 and 1224 BC.

If you want to travel off the beaten path, head to the **Western Oases**. Still seldom visited, they include Kharga, Dakhla, Farafra, Bahariyya and Siwa, peaceful settlements wreathed in surreal beauty. **Desert safaris** via four-wheel-drive vehicle can be arranged.

Nile cruises are an original way of discovering Egypt. Modern boats ply the waters between Luxor and Aswan. Most cruises comprise a three- or four-day sail between the two towns, with stops at temple sites along the way. Or you can opt for a **felucca trip**. Visiting the most scenic sections of the river aboard one of these ancient sailboats is an unforgettable experience.

In Sinai you shouldn't miss **St. Katherine's**, an ancient monastery housing 22 Greek Orthodox monks. **Mount Sinai** towers 2,285m (7,495ft) over the monastery. Egypt's highest peak, it is revered as the place Moses received the Ten Commandments from God. It's easy to climb—you can take the gentle camel trail or the 3,000 Steps of Repentance, carved by a monk as a form of penance. Climb up in time for sunrise, but bring a light.

To explore the rugged, red rock mountains and barren desert of the interior, your best bet is to embark on a **camel trek** or **four-wheel-drive vehicle trek**. A popular daytrip from Nuweiba or Dahab is to the **Coloured Canyon**, named for the layers of bright, multicolored stone that resemble paintings along the canyon's steep, narrow walls.

Israel

A land of incredible contrasts, Israel offers a wealth of differing landscapes, climates, culture, history and, of course, religions. Slightly smaller than Belgium or New Jersey, the country is a patchwork of mountains, subtropical valleys, fertile farms and deserts. The transportation system is efficient, and divers based in Eilat can easily access all major attractions.

Jerusalem, the highly disputed capital of the country, is a fascinating and beautiful city. Tightly bound by stone walls, the **Old City** houses the **Dome of the Rock**, the golden cupola of which is the central indelible image of the city. This mosque was constructed between AD 688 and 691.

In stark contrast to Jerusalem, **Tel Aviv** is barely a century old, a modern metropolis with a laid-back Mediterranean ease and the hip feel of a European city. Central Tel Aviv boasts the country's best restaurants, bars, cafes and nightclubs, as well as superb beaches.

A visit to the **Dead Sea** is a must, where you can swim—or rather bob—in extremely saline water at the lowest point on the earth's surface (scuba diving is out of the question; see sidebar below). One popular shoreline attraction is **Ein Gedi**, a lush desert oasis featuring freshwater springs, waterfalls, pools and tropical vegetation.

Stretching southwest from the Dead Sea, the **Negev Desert** offers interesting **hiking** trails in a variety of landscapes, including the basin of the world's largest crater, **Maktesh Ramon**.

Swimming Lessons

As fun and relaxing as it may be, soaking in the water of the Dead Sea can be extremely painful. Wade in with any exposed cuts or scrapes and you will instantly appreciate the phrase "rub salt in one's wounds." The magnesium chloride in the water gives it a revolting bitter taste and swallowing any can induce vomiting. Don't get water in your eyes, either, as it will inflame them and sting. If this happens, rinse your eyes immediately with fresh water.

Swimming in the buoyant water also poses a problem, since one's legs tend to float to the surface. There have been reports of overweight swimmers turning onto their fronts to swim and being unable to flip back around to keep their faces out of the water. A number of drownings have happened as a result.

Jordan

Squeezed between Syria, Iraq, Saudi Arabia and Israel, Jordan is probably the safest, most stable country in the region. The capital, **Amman**, is a thriving modern, cosmopolitan city built on many small hills. It is also home to several good museums. North of Amman are the ancient Roman Decapolis cities of **Umm Qais** and **Jerash**—the latter being one of the best-preserved Roman provincial cities in the Middle East. Northeast of Amman is a string of **desert castles** built or conquered by 7th and 8th century Umayyad rulers.

But the real treasures of the country are south of Amman. Along the King's Highway you'll encounter the remarkable Byzantine mosaics of **Madaba**, the Crusader castle at **Kerak** and the ancient Nabataean city of **Petra**, one of the most

Wadi Rum is a vast desert landscape of ever-changing shapes and colors.

spectacular sights in the Middle East. Settled in the 6th century BC and carved into the surrounding rock, Petra is remarkably well preserved. It is easily accessible from **Aqaba**, the resort town where most divers stay.

Another convenient daytrip from Aqaba is to **Wadi Rum**, a magnificent moonscape of sand and rocks. This desolate, rugged area was a onetime haunt of Lawrence of Arabia. **Camel treks** and **four-wheel-drive vehicle treks** take in the area's major attractions.

Saudi Arabia

Saudi Arabia recently opened its doors to divers but largely discourages land-based tourism. Vast and mostly arid, it is the cradle of Islam. Contrary to popular belief, the kingdom has an abundance of attractions. Should the harsh visa policy soften, make **Jeddah**'s old city your top priority. Highlights include a vibrant central souq and several fine examples of houses built of Red Sea coral. In the southwest, the mountain city **Abha** is the gateway to the dramatic **Asir National Park**.

Sudan

Diving in Sudan is done via live-aboard, and you probably won't be given a chance to visit the country. For good reason, though: Large areas of Sudan are off-limits to travelers due to a prolonged civil war. You might stop in at the time-worn coastal town of **Port Sudan**, where the British colonial feel is still pervasive.

Yemen

Yemen surprises visitors with 3,000 years of history and culture developed during centuries of isolation and preserved to this day. You'll also marvel at the country's unique architecture, built in perfect harmony with its natural surroundings.

The capital, **San'a**, is a bustling modern city that offers a glimpse into the past. Many houses in the old city are more than 400 years old, and all are built in the same 1,000-year-old style. The eastern section contains one of the largest wholly preserved medinas (non-European neighborhoods) in the Arab world. Home to extended Yemeni families, multistory tower houses use natural, dressed stone in their lower floors and fired brick in their upper levels.

To the south, **Shibam** is a tight collection of some 500 mud-brick skyscrapers more than 400 years old. Aptly dubbed "the Manhattan of the desert," the town rises from a slight elevation in the central part of the **Wadi Hadramawt**, a fertile valley that runs for 160km (99 miles), itself a major attraction. Both Shibam and San'a are UNESCO World Heritage sites.

Bird-watching is a popular pastime. Yemen is ideally located on the migration route of many species, and mountains such as **Jabal Kawkaban** and **Jabal Sabir** are prime sites for sightings. If you prefer a good **hike**, head for the **Haraz Mountains**, close to San'a, with rugged peaks standing nearly 3,000m (9,840ft).

Diving Health & Safety

Heat is the main concern in this desert region. Drink plenty of fluids to prevent dehydration. Avoid sunburn by using sunscreen and wearing a hat, and protect your eyes with good quality sunglasses. Wear a dive skin or wetsuit while snorkeling to avoid sunburn and while diving to keep warm and avoid coral abrasions.

Another concern is contaminated food and water. Never drink tap water, and avoid ice and fruit juices if questionable; stick to bottled mineral water, which is widely available. Eat only cooked food and avoid rundown or cheap-looking restaurants. In the major tourist hotels you won't have any problems.

Malaria and bilharzia can be a problem, primarily in the region's African countries. Malaria is a potentially fatal mosquito-borne disease, although preventative medications are available. Bilharzia, or schistosomiasis, is carried in fresh water by minute worms, which enter through the skin and attach to your intestines or bladder. The infection often causes no symptoms until the disease is well established (several months to years after exposure) and damage to internal organs irreversible. Avoid swimming or bathing in fresh water where bilharzia may be present. A blood test is somewhat reliable but may not show positive results until a number of weeks after exposure. Rift Valley fever, another potentially fatal mosquito-borne disease, may be a concern for travelers in Yemen and southern Saudi Arabia.

Medical facilities are sparse in the region, except in developed coastal towns such as Eilat, Aqaba, Sharm el-Sheikh and Hurghada. Fill any necessary prescriptions before you leave and be sure to be up-to-date with all major vaccinations, especially typhoid and hepatitis A, which are common food-borne diseases. Certain immunizations and treatments might need to begin several months before you leave.

The U.S. Centers for Disease Control and Prevention regularly posts updates on worldwide health-related concerns specifically for travelers. Contact the CDC by fax or visit their website. Call (toll-free from the U.S.) ☎ 888-232-3299 and request Document 000005 to receive a list of documents available by fax. Their website is www.cdc.gov.

Diving & Flying

Most Red Sea divers arrive by plane. While it's fine to dive soon *after* flying, it's important to remember that your last dive should be completed at least 12 hours (some experts advise 24 hours, particularly after repetitive dives) *before* your flight to minimize the risk of decompression sickness, caused by residual nitrogen in the blood.

The Dangers of Deep Diving

Deep diving has become somewhat of an awkward subject in the Red Sea. Since veteran divers don't like to discuss it, most of it takes place on the sly. While it is largely experienced divers who take the risks, novices are occasionally lured down by their peers.

On live-aboards the divemaster watches after the novices, while more experienced divers head off by themselves, often to test their limits. These divers may be unaware of potentially fatal factors, such as the vicious down-current that can develop at Big Brother wall or on the face of Shark Reef, the site of several drownings.

Dahab is notorious for deep-diving accidents, particularly at The Canyon and Blue Hole. Both sites have claimed their share of lives. Dahab itself has no recompression facility—when accidents do occur, it's often the trek over the mountains to Sharm that proves fatal.

The southern Red Sea is a particularly bad place to test the limits, because if things go wrong, you have hours if not days between you and the nearest recompression facility. In Sudan, for example, in-water recompression would have to be considered—not a happy choice to have to make.

MARK WEBSTER

Pre-Trip Preparation

Your general state of health, diving skill level and specific equipment needs are the three most important factors that impact any dive trip. If you honestly assess these before you leave, you'll be well on your way to assuring a safe dive trip.

First, if you're not in shape, start exercising. Second, if you haven't dived for a while (six months is too long) and your skills are rusty, do a local dive with an experienced buddy or take a scuba review course. Finally, inspect your dive gear. Feeling good physically, diving regularly and using reliable equipment will make you a safer diver and enhance your enjoyment underwater.

At least a month before your trip, inspect your dive gear. Remember, your regulator should be serviced annually, whether you've used it or not. If you use a dive computer and can replace the battery yourself, change it before the trip or buy a spare one to take along. Otherwise, send the computer to the manufacturer for a battery replacement.

If possible, find out if the dive center you'll be using rents or services the type of gear you own. If not, you might want to take spare parts or even spare gear.

Purchase any additional equipment you might need, such as a dive light and tank marker light for night diving, a line reel for wreck diving, etc. Make sure you have at least a whistle attached to your BC. Better yet, add a marker tube (also known as a safety sausage or come-to-me).

About a week before taking off, do a final check of your gear, grease o-rings, check batteries and assemble a save-a-dive kit. This kit should at minimum contain extra mask and fin straps, snorkel keeper, mouthpiece, valve cap, zip ties and o-rings. Don't forget to pack a first-aid kit and medications such as decongestants, ear drops, antihistamines and motion sickness tablets.

Tips for Evaluating a Dive Operator

First impressions mean a lot. Does the business appear organized and professionally staffed? Does it prominently display a dive affiliation such as NAUI, PADI, SSI, CMAS, etc.? These are both good indications that it adheres to high standards.

Tips for Evaluating a Dive Boat

Dive boats in the Red Sea can be anything from fragile skiffs to elegant live-aboards. Before departure, take a good look at the vessel. A well-outfitted dive boat has communication with onshore services. It also carries oxygen, a recall device and a first-aid kit. A well-prepared crew will give a thorough pre-dive briefing that explains procedures for dealing with an emergency when divers are in the water. The briefing also explains how divers should enter the water and get back onboard. A larger boat should have a shaded area and a supply of fresh drinking water.

If there is a strong current, the crew might provide a special descent line and should be able to throw out a drift line from the stern. For deep dives the crew should hang a safety tank at 5m (15ft). On night dives a good boat will have powerful lights, including a strobe light.

When dealing with groups, a good crew will get everyone's name on the dive roster so it can initiate an immediate search if a diver is missing. This is something you should always verify.

When you come to dive, a well-run business will always have paperwork for you to fill out. At the least, someone should look at your certification card and ask when you last dived. If they want to see your logbook or check basic skills in the water, even better.

Rental equipment should be well rinsed. If you see sand or salt crystals, watch out, as their presence could indicate sloppy equipment care. Before starting on your dive, inspect the equipment thoroughly: Check hoses for wear, see that mouthpieces are secure and make sure they've given you a depth gauge and air pressure gauge.

After you gear up and turn on your air, listen for air leaks. Now test your BC: Push the power inflator to make sure it functions correctly and doesn't free-flow (if it fails, get another BC—don't try to inflate it manually); make sure the BC holds air. Then purge your regulator a bit and smell the air. It should be odorless. If you detect an oily or otherwise bad smell, try a different tank, then start searching for another operator.

DAN

Divers Alert Network (DAN) is an international membership association of individuals and organizations sharing a common interest in diving and safety. It includes DAN Europe and DAN Southeast Asia and Pacific (DAN SEAP), autonomous nonprofit organizations based in Italy and Australia, respectively. DAN operates a 24-hour diving emergency hot line. DAN Europe members should call ☎ +41 1 383 1111. DAN SEAP members should call ☎ +61 8 8212 9242. DAN America members should call ☎ 919-684-8111 or ☎ 919-684-4DAN (-4326). The latter accepts collect calls in a dive emergency.

Though DAN does not directly provide medical care, it does give advice on early treatment, evacuation and hyperbaric treatment of diving-related injuries. Divers should contact DAN as soon as a diving emergency is suspected.

DAN membership is reasonably priced and includes DAN TravelAssist, a benefit that covers medical air evacuation from anywhere in the world for any illness or injury. For a small additional fee, divers can get secondary insurance coverage for decompression illness. For membership details, contact DAN at ☎ 800-446-2671 in the U.S. or ☎ 919-684-2948 elsewhere. DAN can also be reached at www.diversalertnetwork.org.

Medical & Recompression Facilities

There is no middle ground in terms of medical infrastructure in the Red Sea region. Eilat, Aqaba, Hurghada, El Gouna and Sharm el-Sheikh boast modern facilities and recompression chambers, whereas the rest of the area is virtually devoid of proper facilities. In modern hospitals most doctors speak English.

Be especially cautious if you embark on a live-aboard trip, since some of the sites are quite remote and may be far from any doctor, let alone a hospital. All boats should carry oxygen and a first-aid kit—make sure yours does. Dive safely and avoid decompression dives.

The following hospitals are among the most reputable. All have highly qualified teams of medical experts on hand to deal with a variety of illnesses and accidents.

Medical Contacts

Egypt

El Gouna Hospital & Chamber
☎ 065 580 012–017
emergency line ☎ 065 580 011

Hurghada Naval Hyperbaric & Emergency Medical Center
☎ 065 449 150/151

Hyperbaric Medical Center
Sharm el-Sheikh
☎ 069 660 922/923, 012 212 4292

Sharm el-Sheikh International Hospital (Pyramids Hospital)
☎ 069 660 894

Israel

Yoseftel Hospital
Eilat
☎ 07 635 8011

Jordan

Princess Haya Hospital
Aqaba
☎ 03 201 4111

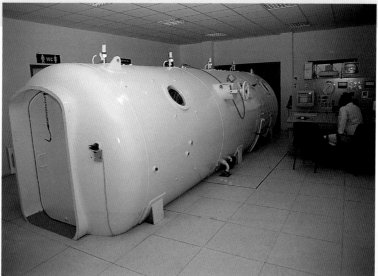

While Sharm's recompression chamber is quite modern, facilities elsewhere are lacking.

Diving in the Red Sea

JEAN-BERNARD CARILLET

Remarkable diversity is what makes diving in the Red Sea unique. You'll find dazzling reefs and drop-offs awash in shoals of reef species and schooling pelagics, all in a beautiful setting, where the reds and golds of the mountains and desert meet the deep blue sea.

Another draw is the wrecks. Over the years warfare and shallow reefs have claimed many ships. Others have been sunk as artificial reefs, including warships, freighters and even a Russian tank.

Not only are the dives varied, so are the means to access them. Several operators use four-wheel-drive vehicles to reach remote shore sites. But as a number of sites are well off-road, camels are sometimes the only option. Dive gear is stacked onto the animals, you clamber atop, and Bedouins lead the camel train to the site (maximum two hours). Boat-diving options range from daytrips that include two

JEAN-BERNARD CARILLET

The original off-road vehicle, camels are sometimes used to reach remote shore sites.

dives and lunch to long-range live-aboards, or safaris, which last up to three weeks in the most remote areas.

Once limited to the Sinai Peninsula and Hurghada on mainland Egypt, the diving industry has progressively extended its scope. Sure, the number of divers in the north far exceeds that in the south, and Egypt remains the core dive destination in the Red Sea—some would say it is too heavily dived. But adventurous divers who want to escape the crowds can now access dive sites and services in Sudan, Eritrea, Yemen and Djibouti, the sea's southernmost gateway. And new areas have opened up—most recently the untouched coastline of Saudi Arabia. Dozens of top-quality, professional dive centers now operate in the region, many boasting a multilingual staff and qualified instructors.

Certification

The Red Sea is a great place to learn to dive. You'll find the spectrum of lessons and instructional products. Hurghada, Dahab, Nuweiba, Sharm el-Sheikh, Eilat and Aqaba are excellent places to take a course, and beginners will feel at ease.

Look for the most reputable dive operations, which maintain high professional standards, employ a multilingual, highly trained staff and offer excellent equipment and facilities. Most dive centers are attached to a hotel, and confined-water training is done in a pool or at shallow sites close to shore.

Snorkeling

The Red Sea boasts stunning snorkeling opportunities. Nuweiba, Dahab and Quseir feature shallow nearshore reefs, where in less than 5m (16ft) snorkelers will find a bounty of reef species swirling amid scenic fields of healthy hard corals. Offshore reefs and islands are also prime snorkeling spots. In the northern Red Sea, boats tie up to mooring buoys a short swim from the reef, and snorkeling is a popular between-dive activity.

Make sure to cover up to avoid sunburn. Wear a dive skin or T-shirt and waterproof sunscreen when snorkeling. Also remember that conditions vary significantly from one region, or even one site, to another—seek advice from local divemasters before you enter the water.

Live-Aboards

Live-aboard boats are increasingly popular in the Red Sea. In remote areas they are the only way to access sites, while in the north they are a good way to avoid crowds and visit pristine spots. The boats are geared toward divers and offer top-end service and amenities. Trips vary from two-day overnight trips to the three-week epics that typify the southern Red Sea.

Popular jumping-off points include Sharm el-Sheikh, Hurghada, Marsa Alam and Port Sudan. Sharm trips tend to last a week, visiting Ras Mohammed before

JEAN-BERNARD CARILLET

Most dive centers hold confined-water training in the pool of an attached hotel.

heading up to the *Dunraven* and *Thistlegorm* wreck sites. Trips from Hurghada either visit Sha'ab Abu Nuhas or head to the Deep South, generally a two-week trip. Boats from Marsa Alam typically spend a week in southern Egypt, while Port Sudan is the departure point for southern Red Sea sites.

Book directly through a reputable dive operation, especially for trips in Egyptian waters; reserve space early for the most popular routes. For packages in the southern Red Sea it's best to book through a dive-travel specialist or your local travel agent.

The Live-and-Let-Live World of Live-Aboards

JEAN-BERNARD CARILLET

Recipe for disaster: Take a fiberglass canister, pack it full of strangers and cast it afloat at sea for a week in some of the most extreme temperatures on the face of the planet. That sums up live-aboard diving in the Red Sea. Why then do most people who try it come away having had some of the best weeks of their lives?

The first rule is to work with those who control your destiny—in most cases the divemasters. They decide where you'll dive, so if they like you as a group, they'll likely go that extra mile to please you. Conversely, if you don't express your gratitude after a good dive, there is no reason for them to bother. This is true for all diving, but since the guides are penned in with you 24 hours a day, it is particularly poignant on live-aboards.

Practicing good diving skills is another plus. Divemasters usually have favorite sites, and you can bet they are the choice ones—but that's no guarantee they'll take you there. Demonstrating good buoyancy and generally treating the reef with respect will improve your chances. After all, you'd never invite someone into your garden if you knew they had a tendency to pick, trample, kick and otherwise demolish the flowers.

Be realistic about the weather. If your heart is set on visiting a particular wreck, for example, you might well be disappointed. Most wrecks are along the rough, windward sides of reefs, and should the wind pick up, as it often does in the Red Sea, diving will shift elsewhere. Keep an open mind and you might be pleasantly surprised.

Personal hygiene tends to go out the window at a very early stage, so a couple of changes of clothes is usually luggage enough, while razors or makeup can be left at home. In the summer pack lots of sunblock, a pair of shorts, some shades and a T-shirt.

Finally, take a spare liver, or at least a liver-repair kit. Parties on live-aboards typically take place on the last night in a protected anchorage close to port. Often several boats will moor alongside each other and the party will spread. Needless to say, alcohol and swimming don't mix.

Pisces Rating System for Dives & Divers

The dive sites in this book are rated according to the following diver skill-level rating system. These are not absolute ratings but apply to divers at a particular time, diving at a particular place. For instance, someone unfamiliar with prevailing conditions might be considered a novice diver at one dive area, but an intermediate diver at another, more familiar location.

Novice: A novice diver should be accompanied by an instructor, divemaster or advanced diver on all dives. A novice diver generally fits the following profile:
◆ basic scuba certification from an internationally recognized certifying agency
◆ dives infrequently (less than one trip a year)
◆ logged fewer than 25 total dives
◆ little or no experience diving in similar waters and conditions
◆ dives no deeper than 18m (60ft)

Intermediate: An intermediate diver generally fits the following profile:
◆ may have participated in some form of continuing diver education
◆ logged between 25 and 100 dives
◆ dives no deeper than 40m (130ft)
◆ has been diving in similar waters and conditions within the last six months

Advanced: An advanced diver generally fits the following profile:
◆ advanced certification
◆ has been diving for more than two years and logged over 100 dives
◆ has been diving in similar waters and conditions within the last six months

Regardless of your skill level, you should be in good physical condition and know your limitations. If you are uncertain of your own level of expertise for a particular site, ask the advice of a local dive instructor. He or she is best qualified to assess your abilities based on the site's prevailing dive conditions. Ultimately, however, you must decide if you are capable of making a particular dive, a decision that should take into account your level of training, recent experience and physical condition, as well as the conditions at the site. Remember that conditions can change at any time, even during a dive.

Dive Site Icons

The symbols at the beginning of each dive site description provide a quick summary of some of the following characteristics present at each site:

 Good snorkeling or free-diving site.

 Remains or partial remains of a wreck can be seen at this site.

 Sheer wall or drop-off.

 Deep dive. Features of this dive occur in water deeper than 27m (90ft).

 Strong currents may be encountered at this site.

 Strong surge (the horizontal movement of water caused by waves) may be encountered at this site.

 Drift dive. Because of strong currents and/or difficulty in anchoring, a drift dive is recommended at this site.

 Beach/shore dive. This site can be accessed from shore.

 Caves are a prominent feature of this site. Only experienced cave divers should explore inner cave areas.

 Marine preserve. Special regulations apply in this area.

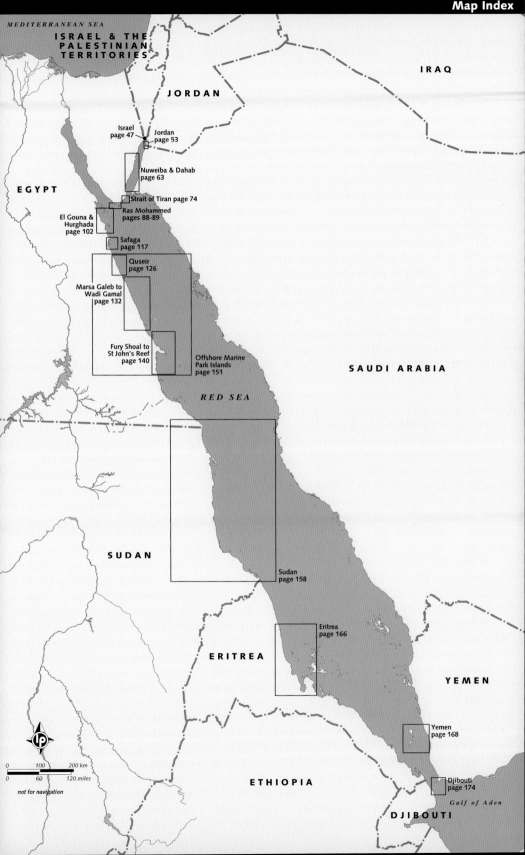

MEDITERRANEAN SEA

ISRAEL & THE PALESTINIAN TERRITORIES

IRAQ

JORDAN

Israel
page 47

Jordan
page 53

Nuweiba & Dahab
page 63

Strait of Tiran page 74

EGYPT

Ras Mohammed
pages 88–89

El Gouna &
Hurghada
page 102

Safaga
page 117

Quseir
page 126

Marsa Galeb to
Wadi Gamal
page 132

Fury Shoal to
St John's Reef
page 140

Offshore Marine
Park Islands
page 151

SAUDI ARABIA

RED SEA

SUDAN

Sudan
page 158

Eritrea
page 166

ERITREA

YEMEN

Yemen
page 168

Djibouti
page 174

ETHIOPIA

Gulf of Aden

DJIBOUTI

0   100   200 km
0   60   120 miles

not for navigation

Israel Dive Sites

Eilat is Israel's southernmost city and port and is one of the Red Sea's original dive resort towns. Divers from around the world have flocked here for nearly four decades.

The town lies along the Jordanian border at the northern tip of the Gulf of Aqaba. Diving takes place along a tiny section of coastline between the city and the Egyptian border, just a few kilometers south. There are no more than half a dozen sites, but each is unique, and all are accessible from the shore. This is one of the few places in the world where you can be guaranteed to dive or snorkel with dolphins, thanks to the highly popular Dolphin Reef enclosure, just south of town.

The diving in this area is different from that of Sharm el-Sheikh. There is little current, and there are many shallow areas harboring large meadows, which serve as breeding grounds and feeding areas for many animals. The gulf waters are colder than those to the south at Sharm el-Sheikh.

Due to the sheer volume of visiting divers over the years, the corals have taken a lot of abuse and are not nearly as pristine as they once were. However, visibility is usually excellent, and

GAVIN ANDERSON

Sunseekers and divers alike are drawn to Eilat's coastline.

Israel Dive Sites

	Good Snorkeling	Novice	Intermediate	Advanced
1 Dolphin Reef	●	●		
2 Sufa Missile Boat			●	
3 Moses Rock	●	●		
4 Japanese Gardens	●		●	

the lack of currents and shallow, easy dive sites make Eilat a great place to learn to dive.

There are many dive operations to choose from. Most offer a wide variety of courses to suit both complete beginners and those wishing to further their dive skills. It is easy to rent or buy equipment, as there are many dive shops in town and at the dive centers themselves.

There are many international hotels, shops and restaurants in Eilat, and there are plenty of attractions for nondivers, both in the surrounding area and farther afield. One popular excursion is a daytrip to the Dead Sea, where you can float atop water eight times saltier than ordinary seawater.

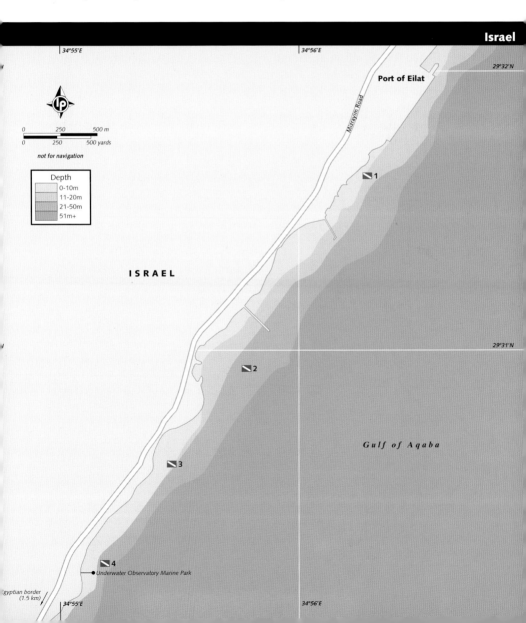

1 Dolphin Reef

Dolphin Reef was set up back in 1990 to study dolphin behavior and seek meaningful interaction between humans and dolphins. An enclosure measuring more than 10,000 square meters, complete with a small wreck and an artificial coral reef, houses about a dozen semi-tame bottlenose dolphins. The door to the enclosure is left open to the sea so the dolphins are free to come and go as they please. Most leave for brief excursions outside the enclosure but always return.

The reef has been colonized quickly, as soft and hard corals have taken root. Groupers, parrotfish, wrasses, moray eels and even a turtle live alongside the dolphins.

Dolphin encounters need to be pre-booked (see Listings for contact information). Before divers and snorkelers are taken into the enclosure, they are briefed on some dos and don'ts, which

Location: 1km (.6 miles) south of Eilat

Depth Range: 8-15m (26-50ft)

Access: Shore

Expertise Rating: Novice

allow gentle touching but no holding onto fins or other type of harassment.

The dolphins do seem to enjoy interacting with visitors, without seeking any reward. Most of the dolphins were born in captivity and have developed special bonds with their trainers. Being able to swim with these intelligent creatures is a thrill for all taking part. For those who prefer to stay dry, there are dolphin shows throughout the day, during which the dolphins perform tricks, again without any reward.

People's fascination with dolphins takes pure form in such encounters at Dolphin Reef.

Making Contact

Dolphin Reef opened to the public in June 1990. Its aim is to study dolphins in their natural habitat while fostering a human-dolphin bond. Although a commercial concern, the needs of the dolphins are always put first. The dolphins are never forced to do anything they don't want to do, and they are never rewarded with food.

The relationships here are based on trust. The dolphins can leave their enclosure whenever they wish, although scheduled feeding sessions encourage their return. A team of research students studies dolphin behavior year-round and operates from a fully equipped on-site laboratory.

The center's dolphin numbers are growing. Initially, there were five dolphins—three females (Dona, Domino and Shi) and two males (Dickie and Cindy). They were brought here from the Black Sea, where Dickie was eventually returned because he didn't get along with Cindy. Seven dolphins have since been born in captivity. The first was Pashosh, in 1993, followed by Shandy, Nana, Banje, Lemon, Yassu and Ympa.

Shandy is the most curious of the group and regularly leaves the enclosure to explore the outside world. But swimming around in the wild holds its risks—hooks in the mouth, tourists dispensing unsuitable food, etc. The center is mounting a campaign to teach the public how to behave when they encounter a dolphin. Above all else, they urge people not to feed dolphins in the wild.

2 Sufa Missile Boat

This boat is one of five the Israeli government ordered from France in the 1960s. In the days leading up to the Six-Day War, the French embargoed all arms shipments to the region, and the boats were held in Cherbourg harbor. In desperation, a small Israeli task force sneaked into the harbor under cover of darkness and "liberated" their boats.

In 1994, in a much more public joint operation by the navy, Marine Parks and the Israeli Dive Federation, the missile boat was scuttled as an artificial reef. The aim was to alleviate pressure on Eilat's increasingly congested reefs. Ironically, the following year local divers achieved ultimate congestion when some 150 of them managed to squeeze onto the wreck, getting themselves a mention in the *Guinness Book of World Records*.

Resting upright and perfectly intact on a sandy bottom at 25m, the old missile

Location: 2km (1.2 miles) south of Dolphin Reef

Depth Range: 20-28m (65-92ft)

Access: Shore

Expertise Rating: Intermediate

boat is great for first-time wreck divers. Potentially dangerous entry points have been sealed off, though experienced divers can still explore the rear hold and the bridge.

The bridge and missile launcher are particularly photogenic, as they are covered in soft corals, some of which have grown to a meter or more in length. Hard corals are slowly taking hold, too.

Fish life is prevalent, with map and emperor angelfish, triggerfish and lionfish. Macrophotographers should look for a group of tiny pipefish, which have taken up residence just below the missile launcher.

Another military vessel, the **Yatush Gunboat**, lies some 300 to 400m south of the missile boat, in 33m. It is considerably smaller than the missile boat and much less colorful, as its hull is aluminum and corals are unable to gain a foothold. However, fish life is flourishing. Occasionally large groupers are spotted on or near the wreck. As with any artificial reef, marine life will only improve with time.

GAVIN ANDERSON

Meter-long soft corals dangle from the missile boat.

3   Moses Rock

Over the years, this one site may have entertained more divers than any other site in the Red Sea. About 100m from shore, close to where the sloping reef drops steeply down from 10 to 40m, a fantastic rock reaches up from 9m almost to the surface. The rock is covered in a wonderful array of soft and hard corals and is home to many fish. Its shallow peak makes it ideal for snorkelers and novice divers.

To find it, enter the water at the café opposite the Red Sea Sports Club and swim along the seabed at 5 to 6m for five to 10 minutes, keeping parallel to the shore. You'll first come across Joshua Rock—not as grand as Moses Rock, but worth a quick look.

You'll know when you have reached Moses Rock from its sheer size and from

Location: Just south of Coral Beach

Depth Range: 9-40m (30-130ft)

Access: Shore

Expertise Rating: Novice

the waves of glassfish that dance back and forth at its base. Lionfish and groupers follow their every move, while moray eels, blennies and many other fascinating fish shelter nearby. Look around the rock for at least two clownfish-populated anemones. Also watch for stonefish, scorpionfish and crocodilefish in the sand surrounding the site. You may get lucky and find bluespotted stingrays. Electric and eagle rays are also occasional visitors.

4 Japanese Gardens

Japanese Gardens is considered Eilat's premier dive site. It gets its name from resident table corals thought to resemble Japanese pagodas. They grow along the wall between 25 and 40m, especially toward the northwest of the site.

Dominating the site is the spectacular Underwater Observatory Marine Park. The observatory tower is about 90m offshore, at the end of a long pier. It stands some 23m high, offering fantastic views of the gulf. Visitors enjoy equally fantastic views of the underwater world through the observatory's 21 reinforced windows. There is also an aquarium in the observatory, featuring sharks and a variety of familiar Red Sea fish.

For nondivers wanting an even closer look at the marine life, the yellow submarine *Jacqueline* takes people on tours along the Japanese Garden wall. The sub

Location: Near the Underwater Observatory south of Coral Beach

Depth Range: 8-40m (26-130ft)

Access: Shore or boat

Expertise Rating: Intermediate

passes the table corals and the occasional group of divers.

There is a limit on the number of people allowed to dive here, and diving is usually done from a boat. Divers are dropped off along the wall, descend to about 30m (depending on experience) and gradually head up toward the observatory. Barracuda and jacks sometimes cruise along the wall, while stingrays and turtles swim the reeftop.

View the pagoda-like table corals on a dive or from inside the yellow submarine *Jacqueline*.

Jordan Dive Sites

There are just 27km (17 miles) of Jordanian coastline between Israel and Saudi Arabia. Much of the northern section of shoreline is paved over by the town and container port of Aqaba, which has damaged the marine environment somewhat. However, there is plenty of unspoiled coastline to the south, between the port and the Saudi border. In fact, this stretch of coast is protected within the Red Sea

GAVIN ANDERSON

While dive boats are available, most of Jordan's best sites are easily accessed from shore.

Jordan Dive Sites

	Good Snorkeling	Novice	Intermediate	Advanced
5 The Power Station	●		●	
6 First Bay & Cazar Reef	●	●		
7 *Cedar Pride*	●		●	
8 Gorgonians I and II & Oliver's Canyon	●	●		
9 Big Bay	●		●	
10 The Aquarium & Coral Gardens	●		●	
11 The Saudi Border	●		●	

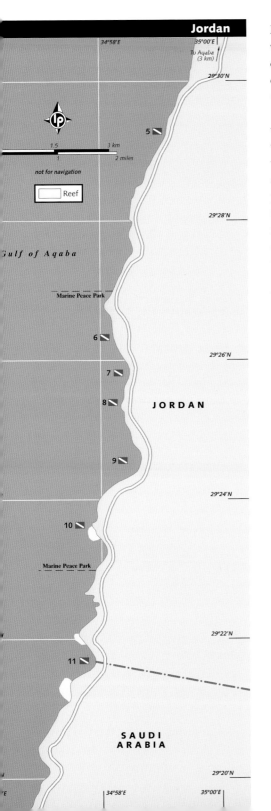

Jordan

34°58'E

35°00'E

To Aqaba
(3 km)

29°30'N

5

1.5   3 km

1   2 miles

not for navigation

Reef

29°28'N

Gulf of Aqaba

Marine Peace Park

6

29°26'N

7

8   JORDAN

9

29°24'N

10

Marine Peace Park

29°22'N

11

SAUDI
ARABIA

29°20'N

34°58'E   35°00'E

Marine Peace Park, run in cooperation with Israel. Reefs here are in excellent condition, and the soft corals, especially those found on the wreck of the *Cedar Pride*, are fantastic.

There are more than 20 dive sites within the marine park, covering a wide variety of habitats, from sandy valleys with coral gardens to sheer walls and colorful fringing reefs. Fish life is particularly varied, with all the usual reef species. In spring and early summer, manta rays and even whale sharks cruise along the reeftop, "hoovering" up great quantities of plankton.

Pressure on the reefs has been eased by the creation of two artificial reefs—the *Cedar Pride*, sunk in 1986, and a Russian tank sunk in 1999. Jordan's King Abdullah II is an avid diver himself and was instrumental in the establishment of these artificial reefs. He takes a deep interest in Jordan's marine environment, which is encouraging for the country's future as a creditable dive destination.

Historically, nearly all diving in Jordan has been from the shore, but boat diving has been available for several years now and is becoming more popular. Be aware that dive centers in Aqaba have different names for many of the sites, and some dive sites are even split in two and given separate names. Needless to say, it can be a bit confusing.

Aqaba has a pleasant climate year-round, although winter nights can be a bit chilly. Visitors take time to enjoy the amazing desert landscape of Wadi Rum, an hour north, where *Lawrence of Arabia* was filmed. The ancient city of Petra also tops most tourists' must-see lists.

5 The Power Station

From a shallow fringing reef of fire coral, a sloping plateau of coral and sand patches leads down to a sheer wall, which drops from 12m to a narrow shelf at 40m. Beyond this shelf, the wall drops well below the sport-diving limit.

If you are entering from shore, it's best to dive the northern part of this site, heading in a southerly direction. Keep an eye out for Napoleonfish, turtles and huge shoals of blue fusiliers, which often cruise along the wall. Also watch for large barracuda.

Location: Just south of Aqaba

Depth Range: 10-40m+ (33-130ft+)

Access: Shore or boat

Expertise Rating: Intermediate

Photographers will appreciate a large outcrop at 22m covered in multicolored soft corals. It is home to all sorts of fish, including glassfish and bright orange anthias.

If you are diving from a boat, you'll most likely tie up to a mooring closer to the site's south end. Here, a short swim along and down the wall to 25m, you'll find rather unusual anemones growing on the branches of black coral trees. Leave the anemones to cruise the reef, keeping an eye on the blue for passing pelagics, but watch your depth—it's easy to roam deeper than you think. Also watch your dive time and air supply, leaving plenty in reserve for your return journey.

GAVIN ANDERSON
In a current, anemones open wide to feed.

6 First Bay & Cazar Reef

After several kilometers of ship, ferry and container ports, the turquoise water of First Bay is a most inviting sight. A shallow reef plateau with miniature lagoons and sandy channels leads to a fringing reef of fire coral and a small coral garden in just 6 to 8m. Here several *Porites* and *Acropora* corals reach almost to the surface. Less dramatic but more colorful are several yellow cabbage corals, where you may surprise one of the local puffers taking a nap.

Location: Opposite the Club Murjan dive center

Depth Range: 5-30m (16-100ft)

Access: Shore or boat

Expertise Rating: Novice

South of the coral garden is Cazar Reef, noted for its black coral trees, ghost pipefish and frogfish—great macro subjects. To the north the coral garden gives way to sand, more scattered coral heads and the occasional table coral. A rather unspectacular reef slopes down from 15m, and it is best to stay shallow here.

About a 10-minute swim from the start of your dive, in some 9m of water, is an impressive coral head covered in colorful soft corals. Here you'll find lionfish, glassfish, anthias and coral groupers. Look sharp to spot a brilliantly camouflaged resident stonefish.

Just south of First Bay and Cazar Reef are **Prince Abdullah Reef**—named after the former prince, now king of Jordan—and **Black Rock**. Both sites are straight out from the government campsite and offer good diving

and snorkeling, with a maze of coral heads and pinnacles.

Frogfish elicit a double take from most divers.

7 *Cedar Pride*

Completely intact and festooned with soft corals, the *Cedar Pride* is one of the most colorful and impressive wrecks in the Red Sea. The freighter lies on her port side at 25m, within easy reach from shore.

On your descent you'll first notice the stern—often bathed in sunlight, it's a fantastic sight. As you move forward along the deck, look for the remains of one of the lifeboats sitting alongside the ship. Before you will be the main mast and crow's nest, adorned in soft corals of every hue and texture. From here more-experienced divers can swim slightly deeper to around 25m.

Following a sand channel underneath the wreck, look for a lovely pink soft

Location: 2.5km (1.5 miles) south of the container port

Depth Range: 10-25m (33-82ft)

Access: Shore or boat

Expertise Rating: Intermediate

coral that drapes down from the hull like a massive Christmas decoration. Moving along the reef toward the bow, you'll find a magnificent garden of sea fans, basket stars and wire and soft corals growing from the wreck's hull and the seafloor. Lionfish and angelfish usually hang out here, as does the occasional barracuda. Fish life is generally excellent throughout the wreck. Residents include Napoleonfish, large snappers and a school of doublebar bream.

Just southwest of the *Cedar Pride* is an excellent site known as **Shipwreck Reef,** where divers often encounter geometric moray eels.

The Making of a Reef

Originally called the *San Bruno,* the Spanish-built ship was renamed *Cedar Pride* in 1982 after it was purchased by a Lebanese company. Just a few months later, as a cargo of phosphates and potassium was being loaded onboard, an uncontrollable fire broke out in the engine room. The fire raged for several days, and one of the crew lost his life battling the blaze, but the ship didn't sink. She was abandoned by her owners and sat in the harbor for four years. No one knew what to do with her. Eventually, the World Wildlife Fund in Jordan became involved, and with the king's backing, the *Cedar Pride* was towed to sea in spring 1986 and sunk as an artificial reef.

GAVIN ANDERSON

8   Gorgonians I and II & Oliver's Canyon

As many as five distinct dive sites sit close together along this stretch of shoreline.

Gorgonian I takes its name from a large solitary gorgonian fan at 18m. From the shore or boat, swim southwest down the sloping reef for five or 10 minutes and you'll see the gorgonian fanning out several feet above the reef. A nearby table coral perched atop a small pinnacle is often home to a yellowmouth moray eel, as well as stonefish and lionfish.

Heading back toward shore, look for a series of impressive coral pinnacles at about 8 or 9m. Each stretches up to several meters in height. Lionfish and coral groupers often prey on glassfish that shoal around the base of the pinnacles. Beside the third pinnacle is a cabbage

Location: 3km (1.9 miles) north of the Royal Diving Centre

Depth Range: 5-30m (16-100ft)

Access: Shore or boat

Expertise Rating: Novice

coral the size of a house. It attracts a large number of fish, from butterflyfish to parrotfish and tiny blennies.

Adjacent to Gorgonian I is Gorgonian II. Here a sand channel leads down to two gorgonian fans—one at 20m and the other, which is almost bent in half, at 33m. On the reef west of the sand channel, in just 8m, you'll find a group of pinnacles known as the "Seven Sisters."

A short swim south is Oliver's Canyon, which features a deep-sided canyon leading to a drop-off at 40m. In the shallows are several pinnacles and the shell of a Russian tank, sunk in 1999. It makes a great wide-angle picture. Fish life is excellent throughout this site. Look for dwarf lionfish, stonefish, toadfish, frogfish and the unusual sixstripe soapfish on the reef, as well as schooling anthias and moray eels on the tank.

Lionfish and a geometric moray eel explore the half-track of a Russian tank at Oliver's Canyon.

9 Big Bay

There are at least four sites in Big Bay, the next bay north of the Royal Diving Centre. The first site is **Blue Coral**, named for a resident species of lacy blue coral. Sand and seagrass patches in the shallows lead to a sloping reef cut through with deeper sand gullies. Fish life includes bluespotted stingrays, which hide in the sand.

To the south is **Kalli's Place**, comprising two small reefs and several small coral outcrops in a sea of sand. Closest to shore, the main reef boasts an impressive pinnacle populated with shoaling glassfish and lionfish, while the slightly

Location: 1km (.6 miles) north of the Royal Diving Centre

Depth Range: 15-30m (50-100ft)

Access: Shore or boat

Expertise Rating: Intermediate

deeper second reef flaunts a lovely overhang adorned in soft coral. To the west the reef drops into the blue.

Farther south, just north of the marine park boundary fence, is **Moon Valley**, a gently sloping reef marked by undulating sand valleys and small coral outcrops. The healthiest corals are found in deeper water.

At the lip of the reef, in 27m, **Paradise** features beautiful stands of black coral and *Dendronephthya* soft coral, which grow along the top and edge of the drop-off. A large grouper often rests here on a sandy ledge beneath a small overhang.

10 The Aquarium & Coral Gardens

Opposite the Royal Diving Centre, The Aquarium is home to two main reefs separated by sand channels, as well as a spectacular fringing reef that sports a wall of giant fire corals. The main reefs drop from 15 to 30m, where you'll find a beautiful table coral smothered in soft corals.

In the shallow sand channel between the first reef and the fringing reef, a pair of pinnacles painted in colorful corals

Location: Offshore from the Royal Diving Centre

Depth Range: 5-30m (16-100ft)

Access: Shore or boat

Expertise Rating: Intermediate

shelter several fish species. This is an

The Aquarium boasts such colorful reef species as these Red Sea raccoon butterflyfish.

GAVIN ANDERSON

ideal place to spend the last five minutes of a dive.

Immediately to the south lies Coral Gardens. Currents are typically slight in Jordan, but this site is an exception and is not really suitable for beginners. Here a sloping bed of seagrass gives way to sand and a scattering of bizarre coral heads at about 14m. The coral heads are dripping with purple and pink soft corals and sponges—multicolored oases of life in a drab desert of sand.

As you glide down the slope into deeper water, you'll find spectacular bushes of black coral. Schools of golden anthias and battalions of Red Sea bannerfish literally cloud the waters. You'll also see angelfish, butterflyfish and lionfish.

11 The Saudi Border

Offering hard-coral formations and dramatic scenery, The Saudi Border is a popular dive. The reef slopes quickly to a wall, which plunges sharply from 12 to 40m or more in places. Here steep walls enclose an impressive canyon. Turtles and Napoleonfish often pass by, as do jacks and the occasional whitetip reef or hammerhead shark.

Head down the wall first, then work your way back to the reeftop, where you can return to the boat from a shallower depth. Look for pristine hard corals

Location: Just north of the Saudi Arabian border

Depth Range: 10-40m+ (33-130ft+)

Access: Shore or boat

Expertise Rating: Intermediate

throughout the site, as well as lush soft-coral growth along the top of the reef. In the spring, manta rays visit this site.

Napoleonfish are among the largest of all reef fish, weighing up to 191kg (420lbs).

Diving in Saudi Arabia

The Red Sea coast of Saudi Arabia extends from north of Haql on the Gulf of Aqaba, near the Jordanian border, to south of Jizan, near the Yemeni border—some 1,730km (1,070 miles) in all. This coastline features some of the world's most beautiful coral reefs, as well as native marine species such as the endangered dugong, a gentle sea cow that grazes on eelgrass around the Arabian Peninsula. Yet few people have dived these pristine reefs, as the privilege of diving here was, until 2000, reserved for residents of the Kingdom of Saudi Arabia. The release of tourist visas to high-end tour groups will allow a new generation of divers to experience one of the great frontiers of sport diving.

On the central coast, the city of Yanbu has grown from a historic port to an industrial city with an international airport. About 725km (450 miles) south of the Jordanian border, the city is home to two dive centers. **Yanbu Divers** (☎ +966 04 322 4246, fax: +966 04 322 7281; hashim@yanbudivers.com, www.yanbudivers.com) is based at the Holiday Inn. The shop arranges shore dives along the coast and boat dives on offshore reefs, including trips to the magnificent wreck of the *Iona* (circa 1915). The 105m (350ft) long ship lies in water 11m (35ft) deep at the bow and 50m (164ft) deep at the propeller. Yanbu Divers has nitrox facilities. Jeddah-based **New Red Sea Divers** (☎ +966 02 660 6368; redseadivers@arab.net.sa) runs the other dive shop in Yanbu.

Seldom dived, Saudi Arabia's Red Sea reefs house pristine corals and abundant marine life.

Jeddah boasts a number of dive operations and has a reputation for exotic wreck dives, including the **Chicken Wreck**, the **Tile Wreck** and the **Cable Wreck**, all descriptive of their cargo. The **Mecca Wreck** is a particularly good shore dive. Some hotels have private beach facilities with interesting nearshore reefs. Dive operations include **Desert Sea Divers** (☎ +966 02 656 1807/1980) and New Red Sea Divers.

COLIN & SUE KNIGHT

Its leathery tube protects this cerianthid from attack.

Jizan, an industrial port city with an airport, is the gateway to the Farasan Islands, which Jacques Cousteau described in *The Living Sea* as having one of the most interesting coral ecosystems in the world. Though there are no dive facilities in the Farasans, a dive professional in Jeddah offers tours (**Khalid Khafaji**; ☎ +966 02 697 6269, fax: +966 02 697 9406).

A favorite site of Farasan divers is **Manta Point**, where the reef is only 4m (12ft) deep. This unspoiled site contains pristine corals of all shapes and sizes and shoals of swirling tropical fish. Hundreds of chromis hover over the coral heads, while thousands of onespot snappers flow in schools along subterranean ravines between the corals. Barracuda often swirl around divers above the sandy sloping seabed, and you may also spot manta rays. Stingrays shelter along a drop-off at 15m (50ft), and large sharks will thrill lucky divers.

Shore diving along most of the coast is worthwhile for the experienced diver. You'll need thick booties for guided walks over reeftops, and a dive skin or wetsuit is advisable, as there is a danger of falling into holes or getting scratched by fire coral in entry or exit surges.

Dive professionals who work along the Red Sea coast regularly experience diving that most of us just dream about. Recreational divers working in Saudi Arabia should contact the local branches of the British Sub Aqua Club (www.bsac.com), whose members can offer local diving tips. Those fortunate few coming to Saudi Arabia on tourist visas can visit some of the world's great reefs at a time when it's still possible to view marine life in its pristine state—a thrill you'll long remember.

Egypt Dive Sites

One of the world's major dive destinations, Egypt has been attracting legions of divers for more than four decades. Hurghada, on the mainland, and Sharm el-Sheikh, in Sinai, have reached Shangri-la status in the diving community. Though these are the most renowned locations in the Egyptian Red Sea, other areas are celebrated in their own right, including Nuweiba and Dahab, in Sinai, and Safaga, Quseir and Marsa Alam, on the mainland. Each region boasts its own highlights, and untouched areas are regularly discovered.

What makes the diving in Egypt so fascinating is the diversity—diversity of locations, conditions, topography, species, dive infrastructures, etc. Though Hurghada and Sharm host the majority of divers, a wealth of options await those with a sense of adventure—be it at remote sites in southern Egypt or on a live-aboard trip. Shore dives, boat dives and even camel trips will satisfy the most blasé diver.

In addition to its underwater wonders, Egypt offers a host of attractions. Whether at the seaside or in the desert, you are never far from cultural or natural jewels that will enhance your diving trip.

Nuweiba & Dahab Dive Sites

	Good Snorkeling	Novice	Intermediate	Advanced
12 Ras Shetan	●		●	
13 Sinker			●	
14 Ras Mumlach			●	
15 The Bells & Blue Hole	●		●	
16 The Canyon	●		●	
17 Eel Garden	●		●	
18 The Islands	●	●		
19 Umm Sid	●		●	
20 Gabr el-Bint			●	

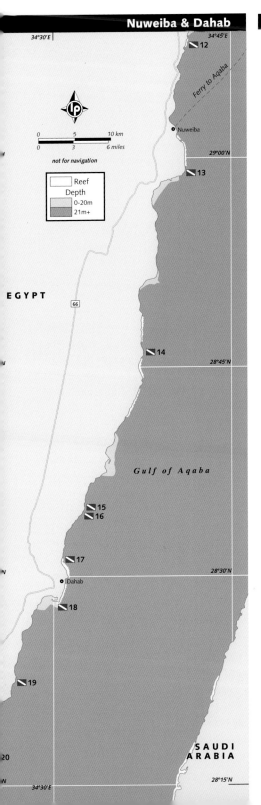

34°30'E

34°45'E

⚑12

Ferry to Aqaba

● Nuweiba

0   5   10 km

0   3   6 miles

not for navigation

29°00'N

⚑13

| Reef |
| Depth |
| 0-20m |
| 21m+ |

EGYPT

66

⚑14

28°45'N

Gulf of Aqaba

⚑15
⚑16

⚑17

28°30'N

● Dahab

⚑18

⚑19

**SAUDI
ARABIA**

28°15'N

34°30'E

Nuweiba & Dahab (North Sinai)

A village beach resort 85km (53 miles) north of Sharm el-Sheikh, Dahab is the wanna-be Ko Samui of the Middle East. Inexpensive camps, hotels and laid-back restaurants nestled among palm trees attract innumerable independent travelers from around the world. Its special feel and cosmopolitan atmosphere can't be matched anywhere else in Egypt.

About 70km (43 miles) north of Dahab, Nuweiba is nothing like its sister to the south. It is strung out over a long distance and has become something of a major port, with a continual flow of people and vehicle traffic on and off the ferry between Nuweiba and Aqaba. However, there are some excellent hotels and nice beaches, and the mountain scenery and reefs are spectacular.

Underwater you'll find varied and prolific marine life, especially reef species and lush corals. Though pelagics are scarce, you may see the occasional shark. The topography is also a strong point, with sand slopes, drop-offs, elaborate coral gardens, coral pinnacles, canyons and shallow undersea playgrounds. Dahab is a well-known dive destination, while Nuweiba remains a bit sleepy. In either case, you won't find the sites as overcrowded as in Sharm.

Unlike in Sharm or Hurghada, where dive boats are the norm, virtually all the sites in Dahab and Nuweiba are shore dives and are accessed by four-wheel-drive vehicle. You'll also have the unique opportunity to travel to some sites by camel—a fabulous experience in its own right. Shore entries are easy, and novice divers will

You Say Mohammed, I Say Muhammad

There is no official written form of the Arabic language, just various systems of transliteration. Hence, common words and names may be spelled differently from region to region. Dive site names are no exception. For example, one of Egypt's most famous dive regions, Ras Mohammed, has several alternative spellings, including Muhammad and Mohamed. This book uses a set of standardized terms, some of which are listed below with their meanings in English.

abu	father of	*kebira/kebir*	big
aruk	several ergs	*marsa*	harbor
erg	pinnacle near surface	*sha'ab*	reef
gabr	grave/coffin	*sharm*	bay
gamal/gamul	camel	*soghira/saghir*	small
gebel	mountain	*ras*	headland
gota	piece or fragment	*umm*	mother of
habili	submerged pinnacle	*wadi*	dry stream bed

JEAN-BERNARD CARILLET

Egypt offers an ancient culture and modern dive operations.

feel comfortable. The setting is also superb. In this area of Sinai the jagged mountains seem to tumble directly to the sea, forming a stunning backdrop.

Snorkelers will have a great time in the area and will enjoy coral gardens in the shallows close to shore. It is also a perfect place to learn to dive, as the prices are lower and the dive conditions optimal for novices.

Desert enthusiasts will find their oasis in Dahab. Numerous travel shops organize trips to the interior of Sinai, lasting anywhere from one day to two weeks. If you have to choose, don't miss the Coloured Canyon, which lies between St. Katherine's and Nuweiba.

12 Ras Shetan

This popular site is easily reached by car on a tarred road that runs almost up to the beach. The entry point is a sandy lagoon dotted with coral outcrops, followed by a wide patch of healthy seagrass. This grassy area gives way to the gently sloping reef. You can head either to the right (south) or to the left (north)—the seascape is quite similar.

Location: About 15km (9.3 miles) north of Nuweiba

Depth Range: 10-30m (33-100ft)

Access: Shore

Expertise Rating: Intermediate

Hard corals are not a strong point of the dive, but there is a profusion of graceful yellow soft corals between 10 and 20m and the usual array of reef fish, including snappers, puffers, parrotfish and goatfish. The highlight of the dive, however, is undoubtedly the contoured topography. Narrow valleys snake their way toward greater depths, while basins and sand-filled depressions and chasms lie between 20 and 30m. You'll enjoy hovering over this terrain, which resembles a smooth mountain range.

Heading back to shore, take time to explore the coral heads and linger around the soft-coral bushes—a good backdrop for photographers. The lagoon is also a safe and comfortable snorkeling spot. An added attraction is a budget camp on the beach, where you can enjoy a drink after your dive.

The Boy & the Dolphin

A few years back a young Bedouin noticed a lone dolphin frequenting the bay off Mizena, a village just south of Nuweiba. He started to befriend her, swimming out into the turquoise water and diving to the depths. She began to turn up regularly and take the young Bedouin for a swim. In the months and years that followed, the two became "an item."

This bond between a human and a wild marine mammal has, of course, attracted plenty of onlookers and eager participants, and visitors now swamp the village in the hope of swimming with the dolphin. To ensure her return to the bay each day, the villagers now feed her. They also charge visitors to go for a swim and to rent a mask and snorkel.

THOMAS HARTWELL

If you do take the plunge, try to be content with viewing rather than chasing and grabbing her. One flick of her tail is enough to propel her away from unwanted suitors, but if the attention becomes too much, this graceful creature of the deep is just as likely to go back from where she came.

13 Sinker

Sinker is a most unusual and attractive dive site. A stone's throw from the Nuweiba Hilton Coral Resort and accessible from the beach, it features a massive submerged mooring buoy designed for cargo ships, which was sunk by mistake in the mid-1990s near the intended point of immersion. Since then it has developed into a fantastic artificial reef, attracting a host of small, colorful species. The main attraction is the truly incredible growth of soft corals that decorate the mooring chain from top to bottom.

Location: In Nuweiba, off the beach, close to Nuweiba Hilton Coral Resort

Depth Range: 6-35m (20-115ft)

Access: Shore

Expertise Rating: Intermediate

Two concrete slabs form the base of the mooring and lie on a sandy bottom at 35m. Divers spiral up and around the chain to the buoy. You'll have plenty of time to inspect the gorgeous purple soft corals that have colonized every inch of the chain, hiding it almost entirely.

At about 20m look up to see the massive sphere of the buoy looming above you. Its base is at about 10m and the top of the structure at about 6m. You'll be mesmerized by the dense packs of glassfish and anthias swirling about, with the purple soft corals as a backdrop. Angelfish and shrimp also abound here. Trevallies usually hang around in deeper water. From here swim back in the blue to the gently sloping reef. Finish your dive close to shore, at a patch of seagrass in 3m on the otherwise sandy bottom.

This site is exceptional for photographers. Hold your shots for the second half of the dive, especially for the sphere. It's a great subject, and you'll have plenty of light.

GAVIN ANDERSON

Soft corals wreathe the submerged mooring chain.

14 Ras Mumlach

This site entails a 75-minute trip by four-wheel-drive vehicle from Nuweiba. The entry point is near a telecom tower. A safe, comfortable dive, Ras Mumlach's ample marine life and attractive topography guarantee a great reward for minimal effort.

From shore you'll cross a shallow sandy area carpeted with seagrass before hitting the reef. Two dive plans are possible. You can either head to the right (south) or to the left (north), though the topography on each side is similar. The reef slopes gently and is interspersed with coral boulders, including excellent table corals. Sandbars and smooth valleys enhance the seascape. The reef gets steeper as you move farther from the entry point, and table corals gracefully protrude from the wall. Some appealing gorgonians also decorate the reef, at about 20m.

If you dive the south side of the reef, you'll notice a large gorgonian intertwined with a magnificent table coral at about 17m, with the expected bounty of anthias flitting about. Napoleonfish, bannerfish, surgeonfish, butterflyfish,

Location: About 30km (19 miles) south of Nuweiba

Depth Range: 10-25m (33-82ft)

Access: Shore

Expertise Rating: Intermediate

fusiliers, angelfish and moray eels add to the cast of characters. It is also a choice location for turtles. Visibility is usually quite good, and underwater photographers can capture intriguing silhouettes.

Keep an eye out for hawksbill turtles.

EDWARD SNIJDERS

15 The Bells & Blue Hole

A technically demanding dive, the abyssal Blue Hole is not a regular site, and no dive centers offer it. The actual dive plan here is fortunately much different and much safer.

The entry point is at The Bells, about 100m past the end of the dirt track that leads to the Blue Hole. The entrance is a narrow breach in the reef table that forms a pool close to shore. You descend through a chimney, exiting at 27m on a ledge that opens to the cobalt sea.

Location: About 8km (5 miles) north of Dahab

Depth Range: 7-27m (23-89ft)

Access: Shore

Expertise Rating: Intermediate

The drop-off is absolutely vertical, and the scenery is breathtaking. As with any wall dive, monitor your depth carefully, as it's easy to unwittingly drop deeper and deeper.

Swim south along the wall. Attractive cavelets and overhangs enhance the drop-off, but the diversity of life is not outstanding. Keep a regular eye on the blue though—you might be rewarded with sightings of a turtle or whitetip reef shark. Ascend gradually to 10m. The shallower sections of the reef are much more abundant in macro life. A saddle in the reef at 7m allows you to enter the Blue Hole and marks the end of the dive. Cross the lagoon to get to shore.

Snorkelers will enjoy the reef's shallower sections, especially over the eastern and southern edges of the Blue Hole, both blessed with healthy corals and myriad fish.

Fatal Attraction

The Blue Hole is probably the most infamous dive site in Egypt. Carved into a reef just offshore less than 10km (6 miles) north of Dahab, it is a gaping hole that drops straight down to unfathomable depths—some say below 130m (426ft). This site has claimed many lives—all thrill-seekers who took unreasonable risks, venturing well below the sport-diving limit.

GAVIN ANDERSON

An archway at approximately 65m (213ft) connects the hole to the open ocean. This is the trap. Solo divers—mostly Israelis who brought their own equipment—have been lured to the depths by the archway. Victims have succumbed to narcosis, missed the archway or been trapped below it, losing all sense of direction.

Apart from its dark reputation, the Blue Hole itself is nothing special, though its shallow outer lips offer good snorkeling. Leave the depths to experienced technical divers.

16 The Canyon

The Canyon is one of the most popular sites in the area. As a result, it's also one of the most crowded. A long, narrow trench forms a canyon running perpendicular to the reef, lending the site its name. A range of dive plans will suit all levels of divers.

After an easy shore entry, you'll cross a sandy lagoon that opens onto a gently sloping reef dotted with coral heads.

Location: Just north of Dahab

Depth Range: 5-33m (16-108ft)

Access: Shore

Expertise Rating: Intermediate

The eerie canyon soon comes into view. It forms a thin cleft in the reef that looks like a winding serpent. Enter at 20m and drop to the bottom, at 30m. There's not much to see, but the setting is striking.

From here you can swim toward shore and exit the canyon through a chimney and past a "fishbowl" at 20m. The fishbowl features a small chamber—in fact, a hollow coral mound—full of billowing curtains of glassfish and anthias.

If you're an advanced diver, you can swim to the outer reef slope and exit the canyon through an opening in the ceiling at about 33m. Exiting the canyon, head south and follow the drop-off at about 25m. Ascend gradually to finish your dive in a sensational coral garden in less than 8m near the lagoon entrance. You'll encounter anthias, groupers, excellent hard and soft corals (including healthy *Acropora* and cabbage corals), Napoleonfish, octopuses, lionfish, glassfish, big puffers and even seamoths atop sand patches that reflect the sunlight. It's a paradise for photographers, who make the most of the perfect conditions, and for beginners, who can train in safety.

GAVIN ANDE

...y through shimmering shoals of glassfish within this narrow canyon.

17 Eel Garden

Eel Garden takes its name from the countless garden eels that carpet the seafloor not far from the entry point of the dive. Though the eels are the main focus, this site boasts other attractions.

The shore entry involves a rather tedious walk across the reef plate to a canyon. At 9m the canyon broadens into a large sandy area that slopes down gradually, resembling a perfect ski slope. Heading north, you'll skirt along a jutting tongue of reef running perpendicular to the main reef before the eels come into view. They wave to and fro in the current like some strange white vegetation. As you approach, the eels vanish into their burrows like synchronized swimmers.

Continue north and descend to about 20m, where you'll find a nearly flat section strewn with coral boulders and several table corals. A dense congregation of barracuda regularly patrol this area. If you don't spook them, they might

Location: North side of Dahab

Depth Range: 5-20m (16-65ft)

Access: Shore

Expertise Rating: Intermediate

circle around you. Big groupers and snappers are also a common sight.

From here work your way toward the reef, which is especially enthralling in its upper reaches, between 5 and 10m. The healthy, wide-ranging variety of soft- and hard-coral growth is rivaled only by the fish life. Anthias, parrotfish, bannerfish and angelfish compete for your attention. Photographers will find no shortage of subject matter.

Bear in mind that if surface conditions are rough, your exit may be somewhat strenuous in the canyon.

18 The Islands

Less than 10 minutes from Dahab by car, The Islands offers tropical coral at its best, with a range of hard and soft corals, combined with outstanding topography. Divers explore a maze of coral boulders, alleyways, amphitheaters, valleys, gullies, passages and bowls in less than 18m. You'll feel like you're in an underwater version of *Alice in Wonderland*.

Divers usually head to the left after the entry point and follow a wide sandy valley before entering the intricate reef system. The quality and quantity of corals is phenomenal, with all shapes, colors and varieties imaginable—from elkhorn to massive *Porites* or delicate table corals.

Location: South side of Dahab

Depth Range: 5-18m (16-60ft)

Access: Shore

Expertise Rating: Novice

Fish life includes big groupers, glittering anthias and jewel-like schools of glassfish flitting around the coral heads. You'll also see unicornfish, surgeonfish, Napoleonfish, lionfish, crocodilefish and puffers. A dense shoal of barracuda usually roams the northern section of the reef.

GAVIN ANDERSON

The Islands encompasses a coral fantasyland of colors, textures, shapes and sizes.

19 Umm Sid

Less crowded than other sites in the area, Umm Sid features abundant fish life and a variety of reef structures.

You enter the water through a wide corridor carved into the steeply sloping reef. Descend to between 20 and 25m and turn left (north). You'll skirt around a massive coral tongue until you reach a sandy slope inhabited by garden eels.

The next feature is a field of magnificent table corals amid large sandy patches between 20 and 30m. The slope here is gentle. Look beneath the coral branches to spot butterflyfish, parrotfish and big groupers. Advanced divers can drop to 35m to admire two huge gorgonians.

From here turn back toward the reef, gradually ascending to about 10m. This section of the reef boasts staggeringly healthy coral formations. Big pinnacles are festooned with soft corals and packed

Location: About 15km (9.3 miles) south of Dahab

Depth Range: 5-35m (16-115ft)

Access: Shore

Expertise Rating: Intermediate

with fish life. Swarming glassfish and anthias run the show. Look for snappers and well-camouflaged scorpionfish. To end your dive, return past the sandy slope and garden eels to the corridor. Spend your safety stop lazing around the big pinnacle at the corridor entrance.

There's not much to see on the right (south) side of the reef except a couple of gorgonians at about 15m that you can spot from the safety stop.

20   Gabr el-Bint

Gabr el-Bint ranks among the most attractive sites of north Sinai, boasting a wild atmosphere and surreal views of the jagged, lunar coastline.

What makes the dive even more outstanding is the unorthodox means of transport you must take to get there. The journey combines a four-wheel-drive vehicle trip and a camel ride. The first leg of the trip, a drive from Dahab to the end of a dirt road, takes about half an hour. Then Bedouin guides will help you perch on a camel loaded with equipment and tanks. From there it takes about an hour and a half to reach the site. The convoy of camels follows the scenic coastline.

The site is superb in its own right. And since it's a daytrip, you'll probably have time for two dives. There is one obvious entry point—a very gentle bay carved into the reef, with no reeftop to trudge across.

Typically, you'll do your first dive on the left side of the bay and your second

Location: About 25km (16 miles) south of Dahab

Depth Range: 10-30m (33-100ft)

Access: Shore

Expertise Rating: Intermediate

dive on the right. Both feature a dramatic seascape, with a steep wall that drops down to about 60m, cut by numerous chasms, faults, sandy ravines and overhangs. Massive boulders protruding from the drop-off attract dense shoals of anthias and glassfish. The drop-off is adorned with healthy table corals and displays of graceful gorgonians, including a virtual forest of gorgonians at about 20m on the left side.

For both dives, drop down to about 20 to 25m and swim along the wall. Heading back, ascend to about 10 to 15m, where a sandy ledge parallels the shore. The ledge is riddled with exquisite coral heads that attract numerous reef species, including swarms of anthias, scorpionfish, parrotfish, crocodilefish, surgeonfish, triggerfish, trumpetfish, moray eels and the occasional turtle.

Given Gabr el-Bint's isolation and the time involved in getting there, dive centers don't always offer this trip.

JEAN-BERNARD CARILLET
You and your dive gear will travel via Bedouin-led camel train.

Sharm el-Sheikh (South Sinai)

Near the southern tip of the Sinai Peninsula, Sharm el-Sheikh (or Sharm) has grown in the last 20 or so years from a sleepy outpost into one of the busiest dive destinations in the world. Divers are drawn to south Sinai by some of the best sites in the Red Sea. Some boast a worldwide reputation, such as the Strait of Tiran reefs, Ras Mohammed and the fascinating wrecks in the Strait of Gubal. Many offer drift diving in fast currents through huge shoals of fish and spectacular coral gardens. Divers here may encounter huge Napoleonfish, manta rays, turtles and even sharks.

Unfortunately, Sharm itself is headed the direction of Hurghada—devolving into a limitless building zone, spreading a blight of hotels along a once-pristine coastline. That said, much has been done in terms of environmental protection. In 1983, Ras Mohammed National Park was created to protect the Ras Mohammed promontory, surrounding reefs and the Tiran island group.

The enforced use of fixed moorings prevents anchor damage and helps control the number of divers visiting each site. In recent years this protection has spread to other areas.

Shore diving was popular in the past, but today most divers choose from among the huge fleet of day boats, which head out en masse each morning to the various sites. The boats normally spend all day on the sea, returning in late afternoon (trips to the *Thistlegorm* run especially long). To avoid the rush, you might consider diving via liveaboard instead.

Sharm offers many attractions in addition to diving. Visitors to the beaches of Na'ama Bay and Sharm el-Sheikh can indulge in a variety of watersports, from windsurfing to paragliding. Increasingly popular are bus or four-wheel-drive vehicle trips to St. Katherine's Monastery or such desert highlights as the Coloured Canyon. Day and overnight trips to Cairo are also possible.

GAVIN ANDERSON

Book early, as dive boats can get a bit crowded.

Strait of Tiran

At the mouth of the Gulf of Aqaba, the Strait of Tiran separates Tiran Island from the east coast of Sinai. In the middle of this channel are four coral reefs that rise from the depths like vast underwater mountains. They are named after the 19th century English cartographers—Jackson, Woodhouse, Thomas and Gordon—who drew the first nautical charts of the area.

The diving is excellent here, second only to Ras Mohammed, just to the south. Strong currents sweep over the reefs, drawing schools of pelagics and sharks. The best chance for such encounters is in early morning or late afternoon.

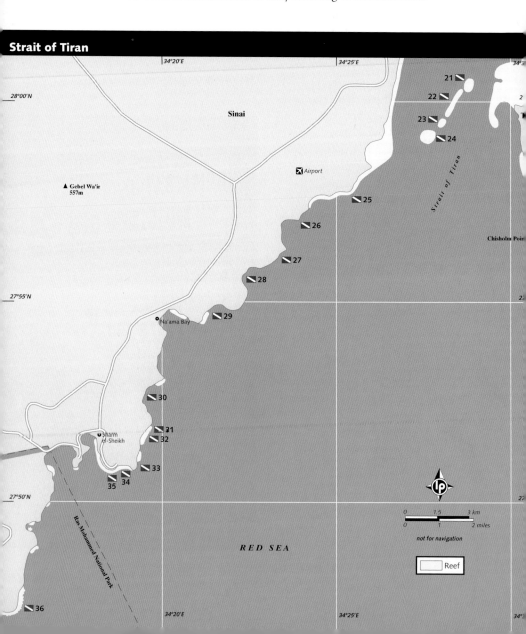

Strait of Tiran

Mountain ranges on either side of the gulf funnel northerly desert winds through the strait, causing rough diving conditions, especially in the morning when winds are strongest. As a result, the reefs typically have a rough windward side and a sheltered leeward side. Diving along the windward sides is much better but not always possible.

GAVIN ANDERSON

Tiran reefs are within easy reach of Sharm's vast fleet.

Strait of Tiran Dive Sites

		Good Snorkeling	Novice	Intermediate	Advanced
21	Jackson Reef	●		●	
22	Woodhouse Reef	●			●
23	Thomas Reef	●			●
24	Gordon Reef	●		●	
25	Ras Nasrani	●		●	
26	Ras Bob	●	●		
27	White Knights	●		●	
28	Shark Bay	●		●	
29	The Gardens	●		●	
30	The Tower	●		●	
31	Pinky's Wall	●		●	
32	Amphoras & Turtle Bay	●	●		
33	Ras Umm Sid & Paradise	●		●	
34	The Temple	●	●		
35	Ras Katy	●	●		
36	Ras Ghozlani	●		●	

21 Jackson Reef

The northernmost of the Tiran reefs, Jackson is crowned with the remains of a Cypriot freighter, the *Lara*, which ran aground here in 1985. Below the surface, sheer walls surround the reef on all sides, except to the south. Here a shallow plateau leads to a saddle that joins neighboring Woodhouse Reef. When a current is running, this is an advanced dive.

Location: Strait of Tiran

Depth Range: Surface-40m+ (130ft+)

Access: Boat or live-aboard

Expertise Rating: Intermediate

There are a few ways to dive Jackson Reef. The most common dive plan starts from sheltered moorings on the south side of the reef. Keeping the reef to your right, you swim toward the plateau. Look for several healthy gorgonians at 20m.

The plateau is the most interesting part of the dive. The corals are fantastic and the fish life profuse. Orange and purple anthias swarm to and fro as danger looms and subsides. Lyretail and coral groupers, redtooth triggerfish, boxfish, parrotfish and broomtail wrasses are all common here. It's advisable not to venture too far along the plateau, as you'll start to feel a strong current, sometimes strong enough to sweep you right off the reef.

As you head back toward the boat, look for a wide sandy area atop the plateau. Spectacular fire corals thrive here, and on the sand you may find scorpionfish, stonefish and, if you visit early in the morning, sleeping whitetip reef sharks. Turtles also make an appearance.

When dive conditions allow, an alternative approach is the classic Jackson drift, heading northeast with the wall to your left. You're more likely to see sharks along this side, including hammerheads—often seen in the early morning and late afternoon, especially in July and August.

MARK WEBSTER

A hawksbill forages for food in the reef crevices.

Know Your Current Events

MARK WEBSTER

It's a barely visible factor, but a current can mean the difference between a mellow, relaxing drift and half an hour of slogging hard and going nowhere. If you're diving from a mooring, you'll have to return to the boat, and assessing the current will help you avoid a long surface swim. If you're planning a drift dive, determining the direction of the current makes it possible for the boat to follow you. Ignore the current and you may find yourself drifting at the surface a long time before the captain figures out what's happened and comes looking.

The Red Sea comes with its own indicator for currents—the tiny golden anthias that line every reef. They always face *into* the oncoming current. Take note, as they have the potential to save your life. Nowhere is this more important than at Ras Mohammed, where vicious down-currents can develop, plunging you from 20 to 50m (65-165ft) in a matter of seconds. Jackson Reef and Big Brother pose similar threats. If the anthias along a wall are frantically swimming upward but going nowhere, then the current is taking them down. Time for you to take evasive action and head out into the blue.

Currents are also visible from the surface. Where they sweep up from a reef out to sea, they create a plume of smooth water at the surface. Likewise, wrecks and seamounts often force the current up and over them. Learning these signs takes many days of studying the ocean's surface.

22 Woodhouse Reef

The narrowest of the strait's four reefs, Woodhouse is a good drift dive featuring excellent corals and frequent pelagic encounters. It offers no shelter to boats and can only be dived in good weather. Less experienced divers should hold out for perfect conditions.

The east side is the most colorful, especially toward the northern tip. Start your dive two-thirds of the way down the reef. Here a wide sandy canyon opens up below you in 30m, a good place to spot eagle rays or resting leopard and whitetip reef sharks.

From the edge of the canyon, continue north along a sandy ledge known as "The Sandy Road." It leads to the corner of the

Location: Between Jackson and Thomas Reefs

Depth Range: Surface-40m+ (130ft+)

Access: Boat or live-aboard

Expertise Rating: Advanced

reef and the saddle that joins Jackson Reef. Beware the current atop the slope of the saddle, as well as a circular eddy that sometimes churns the water. Local divers dub this point "The Washing Machine."

23 Thomas Reef

Thomas Reef is the smallest and most spectacular of the Tiran reefs. Its walls plunge away steeply on all sides, and corals and fish life are abundant. The east and north walls are the best, sprouting whip corals, gorgonians and beautiful *Dendronephthya* soft corals. It's possible to circumnavigate Thomas, though the current usually makes that difficult. Again, less experienced divers should wait for perfect conditions.

Like Woodhouse, Thomas is treated as a drift dive, and conditions must be

Location: Between Thomas and Gordon Reefs

Depth Range: Surface-40m+ (130ft+)

Access: Boat or live-aboard

Expertise Rating: Advanced

favorable. Many pelagics cruise the walls, so keep an eye on the blue as you drift along. On early morning and afternoon dives you may see patrolling reef and hammerhead sharks.

Dives often start alongside a sandy plateau that breaks the east wall at 25m. On the north end of this plateau, a deep canyon starts at about 35m and drops well below the sport-diving limit. The visibility here is usually excellent, and dramatic arches are visible in the depths.

As you round the corner on the northern end of the reef, you'll likely have to swim against a moderate current. Here you'll find yourself surrounded by large shoals of snappers, jacks, emperors, bream and grunts—a memorable way to end your dive.

MARK WEBSTER

Soft coral and Spanish dancer eggs add a splash of color.

24　Gordon Reef

This reef is famous for the wreck of the *Louilla*, which sits atop the north end of the reef, where she ran aground in September 1981. Another ship has since collided with the *Louilla*, splitting her in two, but she remains an impressive sight.

On the south side of Gordon is a wide plateau between 10 and 24m. Seeking shelter from rough conditions, many boats moor here. Drift dives are possible along the east side when the current is running north and along the west side when it's running south, entering just below the wreck. But the most popular option is to dive from the mooring, exploring the southern plateau.

There are two or three routes to take. Heading southwest, you'll find a large circular depression known as "The Amphitheater," or "Shark Pool." Look for sleeping whitetip reef sharks here early in the morning. Farther on you'll find old cables and metal bars—cargo from a ship that hit the reef but survived

Location: South of Thomas Reef

Depth Range: 15-30m (50-100ft)

Access: Boat or live-aboard

Expertise Rating: Intermediate

to tell the tale. At this point it's best to turn around and return to the boat.

Heading east, you'll come to a drop-off starting at 20m. Look for the healthy gorgonian fans at 28m. Continuing along the top of the wall, you'll notice drums scattered along the reef plateau to your left, cargo from an unfortunate ship that hit the reef, sank and plummeted over the edge of the drop-off. From here move to shallower water and head back to the boat.

GAVIN ANDERSON

Gordon is capped by the battered remains of the *Louilla*—a sight repeated throughout the Red Sea.

Starstruck

In the summer of 1998 many reefs in the northern Red Sea suffered from an invasion of crown-of-thorns sea stars. These magnificent animals grow up to 80cm (31 inches) in diameter, with up to 20 arms covered in 4cm (1.6 inch) spines. Each spine is coated with a toxin that is released on contact (see Hazardous Marine Life, page 183). This coral-eating

machine can spawn in the millions on a single reef, each female releasing up to 60 million eggs each breeding season. Adding to their menace, crown-of-thorns have the incredible ability to regenerate from just one severed arm and part of the central disk.

The outbreak was considered so serious that a special body, the Sharm el-Sheikh Diving Union, was set up to assess and act on the situation. The union coordinated resources and manpower from the main dive centers in Sharm, and teams of divemasters removed the marauding sea stars from those reefs worst affected. In one day alone at Gordon Reef, 11 divers collected more than 3,700 crown-of-thorns sea stars.

The infestations continue to devastate the corals in certain areas, and the diving union is still active. The causes of the outbreaks are not thoroughly understood. The good news is that reefs usually recover.

GAVIN ANDERSON

25 Ras Nasrani

Just south of the Strait of Tiran, this site was for many years a popular shore dive, though now it's more commonly a boat dive. The dive starts on a sandy plateau at 6m. A short swim east of here at 12m you'll find a red anemone hosting resident clownfish. Drop down a bit deeper to find sprawling gorgonians.

The current picks up right at the point, where you'll spot jacks, tuna and barracuda swimming out in the blue. After you round the headland, you'll notice an increase in *Porites* coral growth.

Location: 11km (6.8 miles) north of Sharm el-Sheikh

Depth Range: 6-40m (20-130ft)

Access: Shore, boat or live-aboard

Expertise Rating: Intermediate

Look among them to spot the gaping blue mantles of *Tridacna* clams, which thrive here.

26 Ras Bob

Named after Sharm-based divemaster and underwater cameraman Bob Johnston, this site is popular with snorkelers and makes for a good second dive of the day. It is an easy dive, with the most appealing part of the reef in less than 10m.

From the boat mooring drop down between 15 and 20m and head northeast. Work your way back up the reef fairly quickly, as there are several small caves and sandy gullies to explore between 5 and 10m. Here you'll find bluespotted

Location: Just south of Ras Nasrani

Depth Range: 4-20m (13-65ft)

Access: Boat or live-aboard

Expertise Rating: Novice

stingrays, crocodilefish and a variety of other reef species, including masked and lined butterflyfish, triggerfish and puffers.

27 White Knights

In a small sheltered bay with several moorings, White Knights has a number of interesting features, including a deep canyon with swim-throughs, caves and crevices, a dive boat wreck (*Noos 1*, sunk in 1994) and an eel garden. A variety of dive plans make the site accessible to all experience levels.

A small inlet through the reef allows access from shore, though most divers will drop in from the boat mooring just east of the inlet. The reef slopes quickly to a sandy ledge at about 12m.

The main feature of the site is undoubtedly the canyon, which drops from just 10 to 35m. To reach it from shore, swim straight out; from the boat swim south. The canyon is very scenic, carved with caves, crevices, overhangs and two swim-throughs—one at 35m, the other at 13m. Stop beside a ledge at 27m to watch sand tumble down like a waterfall.

To the left of the ledge you'll find the deepest cave, which climbs up rather than back. Look for hatchetfish and bigeyes. Farther up the canyon you'll see the second swim-through. Passing through it,

Location: Opposite Le Meridien Hotel

Depth Range: 8-40m+ (26-130ft+)

Access: Shore, boat or live-aboard

Expertise Rating: Intermediate

you can either head right to see the eel garden or left to look for the wreck, which is well broken-up and lies in 15m.

GAVIN ANDERSON

Caves and swim-throughs lace the reef.

28 Shark Bay

Once an anchorage and unloading spot for local shark fishermen, today this bay is full of sunbathing, snorkeling and swimming tourists. At the north end of the bay are the Shark Bay Camp huts, its dive center and excellent fish restaurant, while the southwest side is dominated by the Pyramisa Resort, off-limits to anyone not staying there.

Location: Opposite Shark Bay Camp and Pyramisa Resort

Depth Range: 5-40m+ (16-130ft+)

Access: Shore, boat or live-aboard

Expertise Rating: Intermediate

To dive from shore, you'll need to pay an entrance fee to Shark Bay Camp. There is a boat mooring just opposite the jetty. As at White Knights, several dive plans are available to suit all experience levels.

The reef slopes away gradually and is terraced with many large sandy ledges, making it an ideal place for dive trainees. Experienced divers will head south to find a dramatic sandy canyon, which plunges to 45m. Don't stray too deep.

Though the corals here look rather fatigued and there is perhaps more rubbish along the shore than fish, this site does attract manta rays (especially in summer), as plankton accumulates in the bay.

Shark Bay really comes into its own as a night dive. Under the jetty you'll find squid, octopuses, lionfish, snowflake morays and the occasional textile cone shell.

Snowflake morays emerge at night to hunt for crabs beneath the jetty.

29 The Gardens

This has been a popular dive site for many years. There are actually three sites in one, each named for its respective proximity to Na'ama Bay. The closest to Na'ama is Near Garden, followed by Middle Garden and finally Far Garden. The first two are suitable for all divers, while Far Garden's strong currents should be left to experienced divers.

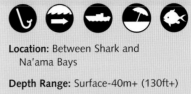

Location: Between Shark and Na'ama Bays

Depth Range: Surface-40m+ (130ft+)

Access: Shore, boat or live-aboard

Expertise Rating: Intermediate

As the sites are just offshore from the hotels, snorkeling is very popular here. Dive traffic and debris from construction have damaged the corals somewhat, though fish life is still quite good.

Near Garden is home to a lovely chain of pinnacles, which extend from the southeast corner of the site. To reach them from the boat mooring, keep the reef to your left and swim out about five minutes. Look for glassfish, triggerfish, bluespotted stingrays and the occasional Napoleonfish. Pay attention to the current here, as it can become quite strong, and watch for glass-bottomed boats when surfacing.

Middle Garden lies straight out from the Hyatt Regency Resort. The boat moorings often fill up at lunchtime, especially on rough days, as the anchorage is sheltered from the wind. Dives usually start on a large sandy plateau near the moorings. To the east the plateau narrows to a sandy path overlooking coral pinnacles and a drop-off.

Far Garden lies 1km north of Na'ama Bay and is the most colorful of the trio. A sandy slope dotted with coral outcrops descends to around 25m, where there are a number of pinnacles, before you reach a steep drop-off. The pinnacles are adorned with soft and hard corals and attract many reef species, including fusiliers, lionfish and sergeants.

The headland at Far Garden is swept by strong currents, which attract passing pelagics. There is also a lovely overhang between 35 and 45m nicknamed "The Cathedral." Due to the currents and distance from the moorings, it is best to drift dive in this area.

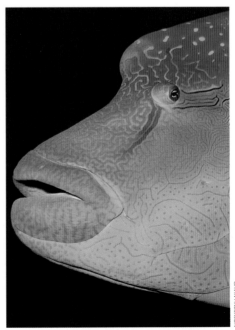

GAVIN ANDERSON

Divers often befriend massive Napoleonfish.

30 The Tower

Named for the tower of fossilized coral that rises from the water on the south side of the bay, this site features a deep canyon with walls that drop below 120m. The site offers highlights for divers of all levels and is a popular spot for night diving.

Location: Just south of Na'ama Bay

Depth Range: 12-30m (39-100ft)

Access: Shore, boat or live-aboard

Expertise Rating: Intermediate

Shore access is via the Tower Club Tourist Village, though this site is more often dived by boat. Dives typically start from the boat mooring in 30m on the north side of the bay, following the drop-off northward. Between 30 and 15m you'll find some beautiful coral pinnacles. Exploring the deepest first, head up toward the shallower section of the reef.

Here you can explore several small caves, home to glassfish, lionfish and bigeyes. You'll see a good variety of reef fish, including butterflyfish, parrotfish, puffers, groupers and scorpionfish. Also watch for the occasional passing jacks and barracuda.

31 Pinky's Wall

Named for its lovely displays of delicate pink alcyonarian corals, Pinky's Wall is an excellent drift dive. Surprisingly, the site is not often dived. The wall plummets well below the sport-diving limit, so good buoyancy skills are a must.

Location: Between Na'ama Bay and Ras Umm Sid

Depth Range: Surface-40m+ (130ft+)

Access: Boat or live-aboard

Expertise Rating: Intermediate

GAVIN ANDERSON

It's best to stay around 15m, where you'll find the majority of soft corals. These vibrant corals make beautiful subjects for underwater photographers. If you bring your camera, get beneath the corals and shoot up toward the sun.

As you swim along the wall, look for a series of unusual gullies that look a bit like organ pipes. If the current is strong, it's possible to drift right into Amphoras.

32 Amphoras & Turtle Bay

Named after the resident wreck of a 17th century ship that once held amphoras filled with mercury, this site is renowned for its history and topography.

The reef slopes away moderately from a mini-wall, which drops down to about 10 to 12m. Though sections of the reef have suffered from crown-of-thorns sea star attacks and diver abuse, there are plenty of healthy outcrops featuring big *Acropora* corals and giant gorgonians.

At 28m you can see part of the anchor from the ancient wreck. Look closely to find remains of amphoras scattered along the reef. Continuing south along the reef, you'll find another, more-modern anchor and chain at around 24m. Fish life thrives at this site, with map angelfish, masked butterflyfish, parrotfish and many puffers.

Leaving Amphoras, you'll drift into Turtle Bay. Here the reef slopes from 9 to 25m. Less trafficked than surrounding sites, this is good place to get away from the crowds in high season. You'll spot pairs of bannerfish and masked butterflyfish, parrotfish and scribbled filefish.

Location: Just north of Ras Umm Sid

Depth Range: 10-35m (33-115ft)

Access: Shore, boat or live-aboard

Expertise Rating: Intermediate

GAVIN ANDERSON

Masked butterflyfish pair for life.

33 Ras Umm Sid & Paradise

Ras Umm Sid is one of the best dive sites in the area, featuring a spectacular gorgonian forest along a dramatic drop-off. This site has been a popular shore dive for years, though now it's more commonly dived by boat. The current usually runs north-south, so if you are diving from shore, plan your dive at slack tide, when the current is very slight.

The best way to dive this site is to drop in just west of the headland and explore

Location: Opposite African Divers and Hotel Royal Paradise

Depth Range: 15-40m+ (50-130ft+)

Access: Shore, boat or live-aboard

Expertise Rating: Intermediate

the gorgonians before drifting around the point into neighboring Paradise. As you pass the fans, look for large groupers, which visit the local cleaning stations, and for longnose hawkfish, which shelter among the fans. Pelagics such as jacks, grunts and barracuda often gather at the point. Manta rays also cruise by, and every so often a whale shark will appear.

Once you've arrived in Paradise, stay between 12 and 16m, where you'll spot exceptionally colorful coral heads, with pink, orange and purple soft corals draping impressive *Acropora* corals. Along the gently sloping reef you'll see angelfish, puffers and parrotfish, and if you scan the sand patches, you may spot camouflaged crocodilefish or stonefish.

A Red Sea coralgrouper waits patiently at the cleaning station amid the sea fans.

34 The Temple

The Temple is one of the busiest sites in the area for training dives. A large pinnacle split down the middle towers up from 16m to just beneath the surface in the middle of a large bay. It is surrounded by several smaller, less dramatic pinnacles, which lie scattered on a fairly flat reef that slopes away gradually to 20m.

In the past this site boasted beautiful corals and giant sea fans, but the corals have suffered badly from years of abuse. Still, there is plenty to see, including big moray eels, lionfish and bannerfish. The best life thrives in just a few meters

Location: Between Ras Umm Sid and Ras Katy

Depth Range: 3-20m (10-65ft)

Access: Shore, boat or live-aboard

Expertise Rating: Novice

of water, and snorkelers will spot many different species on top of the pinnacles, including leopard blennies. The Temple is also a great place for night diving.

35 Ras Katy

Named after the girlfriend of Bob John-ston, a well-known local divemaster and underwater cameraman, Ras Katy (or Cathy) is just west of The Temple dive site. It is a popular place, especially at lunchtime, as there are several shelter-ed moorings.

A sloping plateau drops gradually from 5 to 18m. Head southwest to find three pinnacles, the first rising up to just beneath the surface. The pinnacles shel-ter many species of reef fish, including butterflyfish, glassfish, bigeyes and many shoaling anthias. On the surrounding

Location: West of Ras Umm Sid

Depth Range: 5-20m (16-65ft)

Access: Shore, boat or live-aboard

Expertise Rating: Novice

sand look for crocodilefish, bluespotted stingrays and scorpionfish.

On a rising tide there may be a mod-erate current running north-south, in which case a drift dive is the best option.

36 Ras Ghozlani

For many years this site was off-limits to divers, and it's still seldom visited. As a result, the marine life is superb, with healthy gorgonians, table corals and a variety of coral heads adorned with lush soft corals. Fish life is also exceptional, with just about every conceivable reef species. Drift diving is the norm, as boats typically don't moor here.

A sheer wall drops down to 16m, where a sloping reef drops off gradually at first, then more sharply the deeper you go. It's a magical dive. You'll feel like you're flying as you drift over the gor-gonians. Your chances of spotting a whitetip reef shark are good, and you may also find turtles and large Napoleonfish.

Location: North lip of the mouth of Marsa Bareika

Depth Range: 16-40m+ (53-130ft+)

Access: Boat or live-aboard

Expertise Rating: Intermediate

GAVIN ANDERSON

This lively, colorful reef has thrived in the absence of divers.

Ras Mohammed

At the tip of Sinai, where the Gulfs of Suez and Aqaba meet, Ras Mohammed is regarded as one of the most exciting dive regions in the world. It's best to visit sites early in the morning, ideally on a live-aboard, before the rush of day boats arrive from Sharm. Diving at Ras Mohammed carries a U.S. $5 entry fee for each diver.

Strong currents sweep down from both gulfs, bringing nutrient-rich waters and huge shoals of fish. Schools of snappers, jacks, unicornfish, batfish and barracuda congregate in the thousands in the summer months. Stalking them are the sharks—silkies, greys and occasionally hammerheads and oceanic whitetips.

GAVIN ANDERSON
Divers here encounter solid walls of fish.

Just south of the peninsula, the sea drops more than 2,000m (6,500 feet) into the East African Rift. Most of the fish and shark activity centers around two spectacular towering reefs, Shark and Jolande, which climb out of this abyss and stretch almost to the surface. The neighboring sites of Shark Observatory, Ras Za'atir and Jackfish Alley also see some action, but nothing compared to the main reefs.

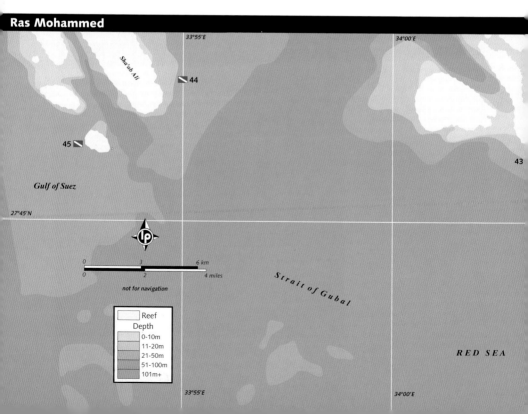

Ras Mohammed

Sha'ab Ali

44

45

43

Gulf of Suez

27°45'N

33°55'E

34°00'E

0   3   6 km
0   2   4 miles

not for navigation

Strait of Gubal

Reef	
Depth	
	0-10m
	11-20m
	21-50m
	51-100m
	101m+

RED SEA

As currents can be quite severe, divers should take particular care to watch their buoyancy control and stay off the coral.

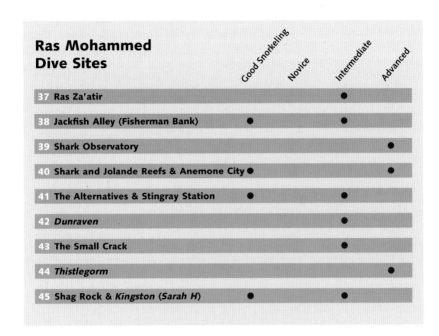

Ras Mohammed Dive Sites	Good Snorkeling	Novice	Intermediate	Advanced
37 Ras Za'atir			●	
38 Jackfish Alley (Fisherman Bank)	●		●	
39 Shark Observatory				●
40 Shark and Jolande Reefs & Anemone City	●			●
41 The Alternatives & Stingray Station	●		●	
42 _Dunraven_			●	
43 The Small Crack			●	
44 _Thistlegorm_				●
45 Shag Rock & _Kingston_ (_Sarah H_)	●		●	

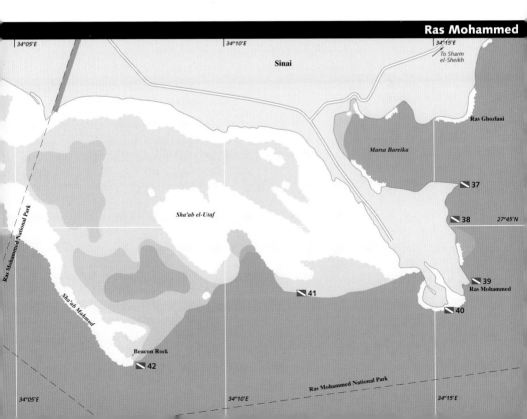

Ras Mohammed

37 Ras Za'atir

On the south lip of Marsa Bareika, Ras Za'atir marks the start of the famous Ras Mohammed wall. It is an excellent site, not dived nearly as often as nearby Shark and Jolande Reefs.

Due to moderate currents, drift diving is the typical approach. The point is the highlight of the dive, so divers are dropped well south of it, close to a solitary pinnacle at about 20m. You'll find a beautiful table coral atop the pinnacle.

A short swim from here, between 15m and the surface, is a fantastic chimney, where glassfish and occasionally Red Sea coralgroupers gather. Out in the blue, schools of tuna, barracuda and jacks busily cruise the reef in search of a meal.

There are many small caves and overhangs between 15 and 30m, where huge black coral trees flourish and massive Red Sea coralgroupers line up waiting to be cleaned.

At the point itself the current picks up and sweeps you around into Marsa Bareika. The colors are most spectacular at the corner, where soft and hard corals compete for every inch of space on the reef.

Location: South lip of the mouth of Marsa Bareika

Depth Range: Surface-40m+ (130ft+)

Access: Boat or live-aboard

Expertise Rating: Intermediate

Ras Mohammed Regulations

In 1983, Ras Mohammed National Park was set up to protect one of the Red Sea's most unique ecosystems. The protected area originally encompassed 97 sq km (38 sq miles), including the Ras Mohammed promontory, the surrounding coral reefs and the Tiran island group. The park has since been expanded to include the entire Egyptian coast of the Gulf of Aqaba.

Visitors to these areas must observe park regulations, whether or not they are scuba diving. Park rangers patrol the region to ensure that both boats and divers are abiding by the rules. They regularly check that boats are using the fixed moorings properly. The number of moorings at each site determines the number of boats allowed to visit the site at one time.

Other regulations:

- Do not touch or break any corals or shells.
- Do not collect or damage anything living or dead, including fish, corals, shells, plants, fossils, etc.
- It is prohibited to enter any closed area and to walk or anchor on any reef, except at marked access points.
- Entry to diving areas is recommended at designated access points only. This reduces damage to the reef.
- Fish-feeding is prohibited, as it upsets the biological balance of the reef.
- Fishing and spearfishing are not allowed in protected areas.
- It is prohibited to throw refuse of any kind into the sea.

38 Jackfish Alley (Fisherman Bank)

A fairly shallow site, Jackfish Alley is a popular choice for an afternoon dive. The reef drops rather steeply to a sandy bottom at 20m with many coral outcrops. Several hard corals and table corals sprout from the wall, but two fantastic caves are the main feature here.

Location: Ras Mohammed, just south of Ras Za'atir

Depth Range: 6-20m (20-65ft)

Access: Boat or live-aboard

Expertise Rating: Intermediate

After entering the water, swim south and you'll find the first and largest cave at 6m. Two passages split from the main entrance. Swim straight ahead into an open cavern, where shafts of light filter through skylights and shimmer across the sandy floor. To return to the wall, take the side passage you noticed on the way in.

From here keep the reef to your right. In a few minutes you'll find the other cave, at 15m. This cave is home to a huge shoal of glassfish, which dance one way then the next as you approach. Look for lionfish and redmouth groupers that hover watchfully nearby. Just outside this cave, at 20m, is a coral pinnacle blanketed in soft corals, where glassfish also gather. Pause a moment to see jacks swooping down like birds to pick off stragglers.

Drifting with the current, continue your cruise along the mini-wall, watching for stingrays and whitetip reef sharks that rest on a sandy alley a short swim south.

Between Jackfish Alley and Shark Observatory is a site called **Eel Garden**, where an enormous colony of garden eels sway in the current at about 20m.

GAVIN ANDERSON

You'll fin through an open cavern filled with shoaling glassfish.

39 Shark Observatory

At Ras Mohammed's eastern tip is a high promontory known as the Shark Observatory, an overlook used in years past to spot sharks in the surrounding waters.

Location: Eastern tip of Ras Mohammed

Depth Range: Surface-40m+ (130ft+)

Access: Boat or live-aboard

Expertise Rating: Advanced

The wall beneath the promontory is very sheer, so this is not a dive for the fainthearted. There are no ledges or plateaus to mark your depth, so it's important to keep an eye on your gauges or computer and watch your depth.

The wall is truly stunning, covered in colorful soft corals and gigantic gorgonians. Sabre squirrelfish, bigeyes and groupers inhabit the many coral-draped caves and crevices, while map angelfish rush around in search of a meal.

It's worth keeping an eye on the blue here, as you'll probably see barracuda, jacks and passing tuna. If you're lucky, you may spot a manta ray or perhaps even a whale shark.

40 Shark and Jolande Reefs & Anemone City

Shark Reef ranks among the most famous dives in the Red Sea. It's possible to see more species of marine life here than anywhere else. Strong currents tend to run north-south, taking divers on a thrilling ride through vast schools of fish and eventually onto Jolande Reef and the remains of the *Jolande*, a Cypriot freighter that sank in April 1980.

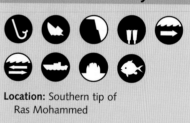

Location: Southern tip of Ras Mohammed

Depth Range: 10-40m+ (33-130ft+)

Access: Boat or live-aboard

Expertise Rating: Advanced

Though boats usually drop their divers straight onto Shark Reef, dives can also begin just inshore of Shark on smaller reef named Anemone City. Here a sloping plateau protrudes from the promontory at 20m. Much of the plateau is carpeted with anemones, which swarm with resident anemonefish and dozens of tiny damselfish. Look for a large metal post covered in soft corals

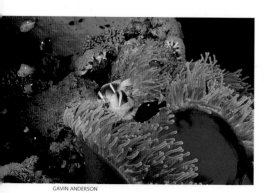

GAVIN ANDERSON
Magnificent anemones shelter small reef species.

at about 14m, thought to commemorate a diver who died here in the 1970s.

To reach Shark Reef from here, swim out a short distance into the blue. You'll soon see a field of gorgonians below you as the bottom slopes steeply away. As you approach the sheer wall of Shark Reef, you'll encounter snappers, unicornfish and batfish schooling in tall tower formations. As you drift toward Jolande Reef, watch the blue water for jacks, barracuda and huge tuna.

A beautiful coral garden grows atop the saddle that bridges Shark and Jolande. Here lush gorgonians and coral heads covered in soft corals are home to huge moray eels, groupers and angelfish. Large Napoleonfish often hang out here, as do turtles.

Divers often finish their tour at the *Jolande*. Not much remains of the wreck, just a few broken containers and the cargo of bathtubs and toilets.

If you have plenty of air left, and if the current allows, you can circumnavigate Jolande Reef or explore another, much smaller reef known as **Little Reef**, or **Satellite Reef.**

Bathtubs and toilets make an interesting if unglamorous maze atop Jolande Reef.

41 The Alternatives & Stingray Station

Seven pinnacles stretching over nearly 3km of shallow reef make this a popular late-afternoon dive with live-aboards heading east to Ras Mohammed or northwest to Sha'ab Ali. The pinnacles are sheltered from the worst weather conditions, and boats often moor up behind them for the night.

The middle pinnacles offer the best diving. In rough weather the visibility can quickly deteriorate. But in calm weather when the visibility is good, this

Location: 5km (3.1 miles) west of Ras Mohammed, off Sha'ab el-Utaf

Depth Range: 10-30m (33-100ft)

Access: Boat or live-aboard

Expertise Rating: Intermediate

is a beautiful dive. The corals are in good condition, and fish life is quite varied. In deeper water on the outside of the pinnacles, you may find sleeping leopard sharks, squaretail coralgroupers and big malabar groupers.

At the west end of The Alternatives is Stingray Station, marked by a large, blocky coral outcrop at 15m, surrounded

GAVIN ANDERSON

Approach stingrays slowly for an up close look.

by sand and small coral pinnacles. This site is swamped with bluespotted, feathertail and honeycomb stingrays, especially in March and April, the mating season. It's also a good place to find leopard sharks and macro life such as nudibranchs.

About 1km west of Stingray Station is a pinnacle known as **The Lonely Mushroom**, which reaches up from a sandy bottom at 15m to within a few meters of the surface. It is small enough to circumnavigate more than once on a single dive. While one side is barren, the other is teeming with life and home to a wide variety of fish. Octopuses are common here, as are big groupers, cardinalfish, sweetlips and turtles. Invertebrate life is exceptional, and macrophotographers will really enjoy this site.

42 *Dunraven*

In 1876 the *Dunraven* was on her way from Bombay to Newcastle with a cargo of spices, timber and cotton, when in seemingly good weather she hit the reef at the southeast end of Sha'ab Mahmud. She split open and quickly sank.

Divers located her remains in the late 1970s, finding plates, mugs and jars of gooseberries and rhubarb amid the wreckage. The ship was later featured on a BBC documentary series.

Today the wreck is encrusted in coral, resting upside down between 15 and 28m. Divers typically start their tour near her propeller, at about 19m.

From there enter the wreck through a gaping hole on the starboard side of the ship's upturned hull. Bring a light, as it's quite dark inside. Swimming up through the boiler and engine rooms, you'll be surrounded by glassfish and staring into the faces of groupers and lionfish.

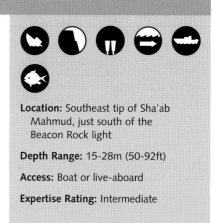

Location: Southeast tip of Sha'ab Mahmud, just south of the Beacon Rock light

Depth Range: 15-28m (50-92ft)

Access: Boat or live-aboard

Expertise Rating: Intermediate

Emerging from another large hole amidships, continue forward to explore the remains of the broken bow several meters farther up the reef. Once full of glassfish and lionfish, the bow is now home to a small shoal of grunts. To finish your dive, follow the current up the sloping reef wall back to your dive boat.

Divers disappear in the blizzard of glassfish swirling through the engine room.

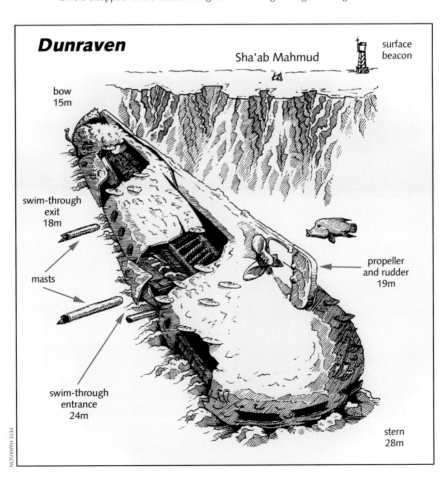

Dunraven

Sha'ab Mahmud

surface
beacon

bow
15m

swim-through
exit
18m

masts

propeller
and rudder
19m

swim-through
entrance
24m

stern
28m

43 | The Small Crack

Sha'ab Mahmud shelters a shallow turquoise lagoon from the Strait of Gubal. The reef is cut through by two channels—The Big Crack and The Small Crack, which only scuba divers and small inflatable boats can negotiate safely.

Dive boats usually anchor in the lagoon, and a Zodiac or dinghy shuttles divers to the outer reef. Provided the current is going north-south, divers drop in north of The Small Crack.

Upon entering the water, you'll find a spectacular wall that drops down to a sandy plateau at 20m. The wall is covered in corals, and gorgonians thrive along the bottom. You'll also find plenty of fish, including colorful boxfish, titan triggerfish (which vigorously guard their nests, especially from August to September) and many species of butterflyfish, parrotfish, angelfish and wrasses.

Location: Northwest side of Sha'ab Mahmud

Depth Range: 5-20m (45-65ft)

Access: Live-aboard

Expertise Rating: Intermediate

Other visitors include turtles, leopard and whitetip reef sharks, schools of jacks and passing tuna.

As you drift along the wall, keep an eye out for the reef passage back to the lagoon, as it's possible to get distracted and fly right past it. The crack starts at about 7m, but it can rise as shallow as 2 or 3m in the passage to the lagoon. The colors and fish life are superb in this shallow water.

44 | *Thistlegorm*

Nearly everyone who visits the Red Sea has heard about the SS *Thistlegorm*. Resting upright on a sandy seabed at about 30m, almost totally intact, the WWII-era British supply ship is one of

Location: Sha'ab Ali

Depth Range: 17-30m (56-100ft)

Access: Boat or live-aboard

Expertise Rating: Advanced

EDWARD SNIJDERS
BSA 350 motorbikes still stand in orderly rows.

the best wreck dives in the world. Day boats from Sharm el-Sheikh and Hurghada leave very early each morning to make the three-hour-plus journey to this legendary wreck.

In 1941 the *Thistlegorm* was headed for North Africa, her holds packed full of military supplies. On October 6, while the ship was at anchor, a German long-range

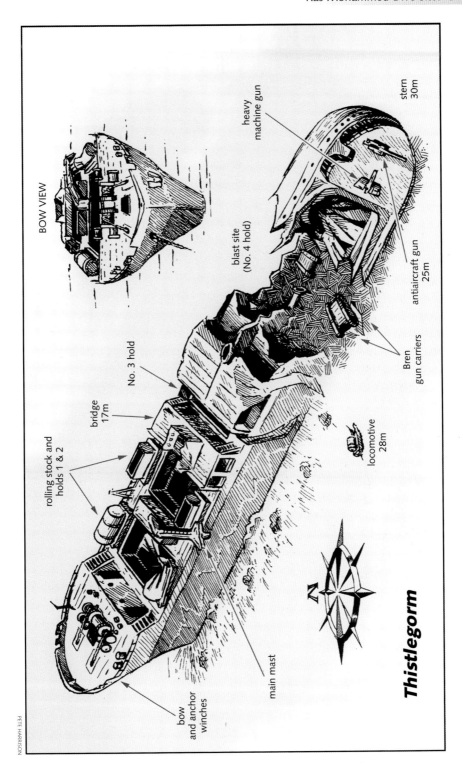

BOW VIEW

Thistlegorm

bow
and anchor
winches

main mast

rolling stock and
holds 1 & 2

bridge
17m

No. 3 hold

locomotive
28m

blast site
(No. 4 hold)

Bren
gun carriers

heavy
machine gun

antiaircraft gun
25m

stern
30m

PETE HARRISON

bomber scored a direct hit on her No. 4 hold. The mines and ammunition stored inside exploded, tearing the ship almost in two. The force of the blast sent the two railway locomotives the vessel was carrying hurtling through the air. Incredibly, they landed upright on the seabed, one on either side of the wreck.

In addition to the two locomotives and their rolling stock, the ship carried Bedford trucks, Morris cars, BSA 350 motorbikes, Bren gun carriers, hundreds of boxes of rifles, fighter plane wings, torpedoes, antitank mines, ammunition, tires, medical supplies and even Wellington boots.

Fish life around the wreck is equally varied. Jacks, snappers and barracuda often ride the current in mid-water, while batfish and bannerfish school on the wreck. Large groupers, parrotfish and various angelfish are also common.

The wreck is too large to explore on one dive. It's best to explore the deeper

sections such as the stern on your first dive, then explore the deck and holds on your second dive.

On the stern deck at 25m you'll find a heavy machine gun and a 39mm anti-aircraft gun. Swimming toward the bow, you'll pass the area of the main blast. Two upturned MK11 Bren gun carriers lie amid cases of 6-inch shells, 303 bullets and a web of twisted metal. Look toward the sand on the port side to spot one of the locomotives.

Farther forward you'll find the bridge and the captain's cabin and bathroom. Toward the bow is hold No. 2, flanked by two large engine tenders. The connected upper and lower decks of holds 1 and 2 are where you'll find the motorbikes, cars, trucks, rifles and boots.

The current can get quite strong on the wreck and usually runs from either bow to stern or vice versa. Make sure to reserve plenty of air for the swim back to your boat.

Bedford trucks are parked for eternity on the lower deck of hold No. 2.

Final Voyage of the *Thistlegorm*

GAVIN ANDERSON

Built by the North East Marine Engineering Co., the 129m (431ft) cargo ship christened the *Thistlegorm* was completed and launched in 1940 by Joseph L. Thompson & Sons in Sunderland, England. She had made several successful trips to North America, the East Indies and Argentina before setting out from Glasgow, Scotland, in September 1941. She had taken on vital military supplies destined for North Africa, where British forces were preparing for Operation Crusader—the relief of Tobruk against the German 8th Army.

At 2am on October 6, 1941, a mere 18 months after she was launched, the *Thistlegorm* met her end. She had safely negotiated the Cape of Good Hope and sailed up the Red Sea to the Strait of Gubal where, along with many other ships in her convoy, she was awaiting her call sign to proceed up the Gulf of Suez.

Four Heinkel He 111s flying out of Crete mounted the attack on the convoy. They were returning from an armed reconnaissance mission up the Sinai coast and targeted the ships to offload their unused bombs.

The crew of the HMS *Carlisle* had a grandstand view of the attack. One of the young gunners, Dennis Gray, remembers being paralyzed with fear at the sight of one of the locomotives from the deck of the *Thistlegorm* flying through the air toward their ship. The planes had come in so quickly and so low that the gunners didn't manage to get a shot at them.

Due to the warm nights, the *Thistlegorm*'s gunners were sleeping on deck close to the No. 4 hold. Most were killed instantly. Some survivors were able to escape in the only lifeboat not damaged in the blast. Many of the crew trapped aft jumped from the ship. Angus Macleay was the exception. He ran across the blazing-hot deck to rescue one of the injured gunners and was later awarded the George Medal and the Lloyd's War Medal for Bravery at Sea.

The *Carlisle* picked up survivors. The men of the *Thistlegorm* had watched their ship disappear in just 20 minutes, slipping under with a protest of hissing steam from her flooded boilers. Out of a crew of 49, eight died on the ship and a ninth drowned.

The *Thistlegorm* lay undisturbed until 1956, when legendary French diver Jacques Cousteau located the wreck. He and his team found a museum of WWII cargo packed in the holds much as it had been 15 years earlier. Cousteau took the ship's bell, the captain's safe and a motorbike but otherwise left the wreck as he found it.

In the early 1990s she was rediscovered by a small group of divers, who managed to keep its location a secret for only a few years. Today the *Thistlegorm* is one of the most dived wrecks in the world and sadly sees far too many divers. There are no mooring buoys, and as a result, dive boats tying straight onto the wreck have torn away large sections of hand railing. One of the main masts has also been damaged, and irresponsible divers have made off with much of the smaller cargo items.

45 Shag Rock & *Kingston (Sarah H)*

At the southern end of Sha'ab Ali is a small, almost-circular reef frequented by shags (cormorants), hence the name Shag Rock. On the north side of this reef lies the coral-encrusted wreck of the *Kingston*—known by many as the *Sarah H*, after the wife of a well-known live-aboard captain. The steam-driven cargo ship sank after running aground on the reef in 1881.

The ship is easy to find, as it lies just below the wreck of a fishing boat that sits high and dry on the reef. Although the *Kingston*'s bow has been virtually destroyed, her stern remains remarkably intact, and she is a very photogenic wreck.

Her twin boilers rest on the reeftop. Beyond them a large section of the wreck stands high atop the reef like Roman pillars. Fish life thrives on and around the wreck. A large shoal of resident grunts

Location: 1km (.6 miles) southwest of Sha'ab Ali lagoon

Depth Range: 8-25m (26-82ft)

Access: Live-aboard

Expertise Rating: Intermediate

stand guard, while colorful groupers, parrotfish and wrasses weave their way in and out of the stern passages and swim-throughs.

The wreck isn't very big, so you'll likely have time left to explore the reef, which boasts healthy coral formations and lots of fish. When a current is running, this is an advanced dive.

The stern of the *Kingston* is largely intact and offers several interesting swim-throughs.

GAVIN ANDERSON

El Gouna & Hurghada

For many divers the Red Sea is synonymous with Hurghada, a resort hub on the coast of mainland Egypt. Though challenged to an extent by up-and-coming Sharm el-Sheikh, it is still considered by many to be the capital of the region.

Hurghada claims the distinction of being the first commercial dive base in the Red Sea, dating back to the 1960s. It's now a thriving metropolis devoted entirely to diving enthusiasts and sunseekers, with some 150 hotels and more than 100 dive operators. The inevitable result is that the area is heavily dived.

Following increasing pressures on the marine environment, including anchor damage from the hundreds of dive boats visiting the reefs each day, the Hurghada Environmental Protection & Conservation Association, or HEPCA (see "Battle of the Buoys," page 185), took action to safeguard the ecosystem, adding permanent moorings to many of the sites.

El Gouna is a fledgling resort town about 20km (12 miles) north of Hurghada. It's built on a more human scale and is far more tastefully designed than Hurghada.

Most of the sites are offshore and involve a minimum boat ride of 30 minutes to an hour. The dive centers provide daily guided boat services, offering two dives per day with lunch on board. If it's windy, the ride can be rough, so be prepared. Be aware that weather conditions, especially the prevailing northerly winds, are a key factor here. The dive operators don't offer a set weekly, or even daily, dive program. They check the weather early in the morning before deciding which sites they are going to visit. Take this into account when planning your trip.

Though it cannot compete with what's offered in the Deep South, diving is excellent, with vibrant reefs, drop-offs and a fantastic, unearthly graveyard of wrecks on Sha'ab Abu Nuhas. Marine life revolves around reef species, with only occasional pelagic sightings. The diversity of coral is amazing, though in some places storms and crown-of-thorns sea stars have taken their toll. Most dives cater to novice and experienced divers alike.

Hurghada is a jumping-off point for extended live-aboard trips. It's also a good place to take courses and a great spot for snorkelers. The most reputable dive centers organize safaris to the north (up to Bluff Point), to the east (the wrecks of Sha'ab Abu Nuhas and the *Thistlegorm*) and to the south, lasting anywhere from a couple of days to a week.

JEAN-BERNARD CARILLET

Hurghada's busy harbor is geared to diving activities.

El Gouna & Hurghada

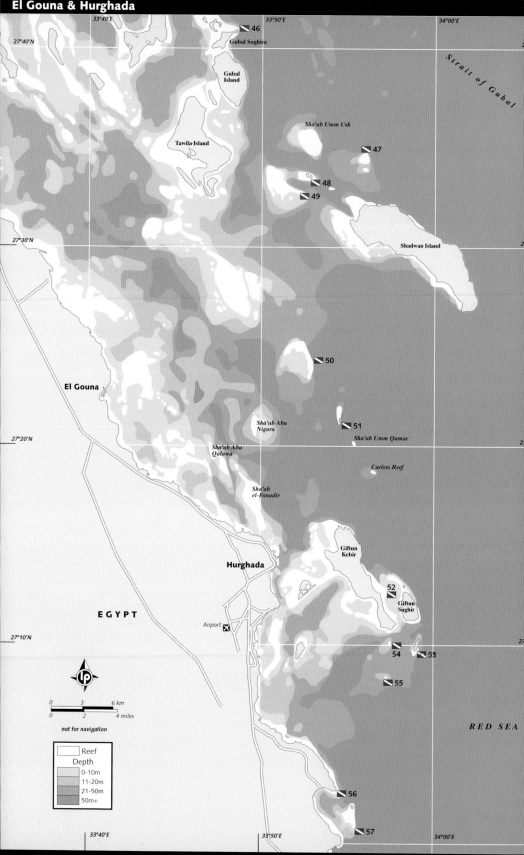

El Gouna & Hurghada Dive Sites

	Good Snorkeling	Novice	Intermediate	Advanced
46 Bluff Point	●		●	
47 Sha'ab Abu Nuhas – The Wrecks			●	
48 Siyul Kebira	●		●	
49 Siyul Soghira	●	●		
50 Sha'ab el-Erg	●	●		
51 Umm Qamar			●	
52 Giftun Islands	●		●	
53 Erg Abu Ramada			●	
54 Aruk Giftun	●	●		
55 Gota Abu Ramada	●	●		
56 Ras Disha	●	●		
57 Abu Hashish	●	●		

46 Bluff Point

The northernmost site in this region, Bluff Point is a favorite for live-aboards out of Hurghada and Sharm el-Sheikh, which overnight in a sheltered lagoon close to the dive area. The site is just east of Gubal Soghira (Small Gubal), off the namesake headland that juts into the open sea.

Current is a major factor here, and your divemaster will assess its direction and strength before suggesting a dive plan. It's usually approached as a drift. Divers are dropped along a steep drop-off north of the beacon—a notable landmark—and proceed south along the reef.

The reef sports some graceful gorgonians and black coral bushes, while

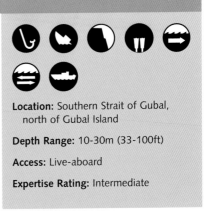

Location: Southern Strait of Gubal, north of Gubal Island

Depth Range: 10-30m (33-100ft)

Access: Live-aboard

Expertise Rating: Intermediate

hard corals are just average. Between 20 and 30m the wall is peppered with fissures and crevices that form an ideal habitat for several species, including lionfish and groupers.

As you approach the beacon, the drop-off gradually gives way to a gentle slope and coral boulders that rise from a sandy seabed at about 10m. You may spot cornetfish, bigeyes, fusiliers, parrotfish, goatfish, puffers and gobies.

Air permitting, you can continue until you reach a sunken barge abuzz with small life, including glassfish and morays. Bluff Point is reputed to be a good place to see turtles, and dolphins are also regular visitors.

Another notable feature a bit farther north is the wreck of the *Ulysses*, a 90m steamship that sank in 1887. A favorite of photographers, its stern is at 28m.

A regal angelfish and anthias dart amid the colorful remains of the *Ulysses*.

47 Sha'ab Abu Nuhas – The Wrecks

About halfway between Hurghada and Ras Mohammed lies a treacherous reef patch named Sha'ab Abu Nuhas. It lies at the edge of the main shipping lane through the Suez that connects Europe to the Orient. Utterly exposed to the northerly prevailing winds, it has trapped countless vessels, several of which sank along the north side of the reef. From west to east there are four complete wrecks—the *Giannis D*, the *Carnatic*, the *Chrisoula K* and the *Kimon M*. Dive plans are available to suit all experience levels.

Northbound live-aboards stop at Abu Nuhas, as do day boats from El Gouna. From Hurghada the trip is more complicated, taking anywhere from 3 to 5

Location: Southern Strait of Gubal, north of Shadwan Island

Depth Range: 5-26m (16-85ft)

Access: Boat or live-aboard

Expertise Rating: Intermediate

hours, and is therefore less often found on the dive centers' itineraries.

Another factor to consider is the weather. The site is completely exposed to waves, swell and wind. Dive boats usually anchor on the sheltered south side, and a Zodiac takes divers to the

MARK WEBSTER

Anthias glow in the darkness of the engine room deep within the *Giannis D*.

wrecks. However, if conditions are rough, the dive trip might be cancelled.

The westernmost and most visited wreck is the *Giannis D*. This 100m Greek freighter once plied the Rijeka–Hodeida route. In April 1983 it struck the reef, broke in two and sank. The stern lies at 26m, and the tip of the crane gantry is at 4m, visible from the surface.

The stern is the most appealing part of the wreck. It is well preserved and can be penetrated by advanced divers—though because it leans at 45 degrees, swimming through can be awkward. Shafts of sunlight filter eerily through its windows. Bring a light if you want to explore the engine room, packed with glassfish.

The collapsed midsection is partly covered with hard corals and home to various colorful reef species, including snappers, groupers, parrotfish, angelfish and lionfish. The bow section lies on its port side. Here you'll find a web of wires,

ropes, masts and winches. Soft corals blanket some structures, and photographers will have no shortage of silhouetted subjects. Batfish, anthias, fusiliers, butterflyfish and even morays add a touch of color and action.

Farther east is the *Carnatic*. Once a passenger and mail ship for the P&O line, she hit the reef in 1869 due to a navigational error. The 90m wreck rests in 25m at the stern and about 12m at the bow. Like the *Giannis D*, she also lies on her port side and the midsection has collapsed. The hull is encrusted with a variety of hard and soft corals.

The most distinctive features are her two masts, huge rudder and propeller. Penetration through the support struts is very safe—a delight for photographers, they form an open skeleton that's bathed in sunlight. A big table coral perched atop a davit makes another good subject, as do resident moray eels. A dense shoal

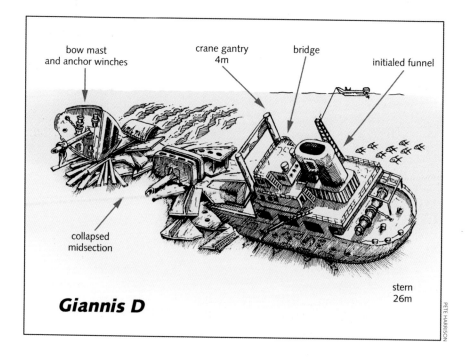

bow mast and anchor winches

crane gantry 4m

bridge

initialed funnel

collapsed midsection

stern 26m

Giannis D

PETE HARRISON

Stacks of Italian tiles lie scattered amid the wreckage of the *Chrisoula K.*

of glassfish also inhabits the wreck, at about 15m toward the bow.

Next is the **Chrisoula K**, another Greek freighter, which sank in 1981 while transporting tiles to Jeddah from Italy. The 98m wreck lies on her starboard side, the stern section at 26m and the bow almost reaching the surface. She is less visited but no less spectacular than the former wrecks.

If the weather is calm, and under the guidance of a divemaster, experienced divers can penetrate the engine room, full of machinery, ladders, staircases, tools, etc. Though light penetrates the wreck, you'll need to bring a dive light. Photographers will find numerous subjects, including the rudder, propeller, winches, mast and intact tiles in the holds.

The easternmost of the four wrecks is thought to be the **Kimon M** (see "Identity Crisis," at right). Not much is known about her, other than she probably sank in 1978—though even that is up for debate. Also less dived than the *Giannis D*

or the *Carnatic*, the ship lies at 24m on her starboard side. The bow lies on the reef, close to the navigational beacon.

Sparsely covered with corals, her unscathed metallic structures look like a huge factory. Penetration is possible in calm weather, though not recommended because the wreck is unstable. Schooling batfish, groupers, glassfish, angelfish and bigeyes usually hang around during safety stops on the reef above the hull.

Identity Crisis

A healthy debate surrounds the true identities of the wrecks at Sha'ab Abu Nuhas, especially when it comes to the *Kimon M* and the *Chrisoula K*. Many vessels lie submerged along the reef, and there is some confusion regarding which is which. This book lists the most commonly used name for each wreck.

For wreck buffs, the debate merely spices up the diving. For more information on the subject, try to find a copy of Peter Collings' book *Sinai Shipwrecks.*

48 Siyul Kebira

Skirting the southeastern edge of Siyul Kebira (Big Siyul), this site offers two dive plans. If the current is strong, you can do a drift dive. The boat drops you on the northwestern side of the island, and you follow the current along the reef. Alternatively, you can start at the mooring buoys at the southeastern tip, tour the reef, then return to the buoys. The upper section of the reef offers great snorkeling.

The reef features a wall that drops to about 15m before sloping gently to 30m, where it meets the sand. The wall is adorned with thickets of hard and soft corals, including several healthy *Acropora*

Location: Southern Strait of Gubal, between Tawila and Shadwan Islands

Depth Range: 10-30m (33-100ft)

Access: Boat or live-aboard

Expertise Rating: Intermediate

Bigeyes hide out by day and feed at night.

GAVIN ANDERSON

species. There are numerous sand patches between 15 and 30m, and several massive coral outcrops dot the reef, including a lush one at 8m, close to the buoy, and a U-shaped cluster at about 20m. The latter sports a huge gorgonian and a pristine table coral, surrounded by packs of anthias and glassfish.

In the first 10m along the reef you'll find bannerfish, angelfish, bigeyes, lionfish, morays, groupers, triggerfish, parrotfish, surgeonfish, bluespotted stingrays, goatfish and snappers. Keep an eye on the open water for the occasional passing turtle, whitetip reef shark or hunting trevallies. Leopard sharks often rest on the seabed.

49 Siyul Soghira

Siyul Soghira (Small Siyul) has a fairly similar profile to Siyul Kebira. A drift dive is the norm if a current is flowing. The site is along the north side of a fingerlike reef that points east into the open sea. This is a safe, easy dive, and snorkelers will have plenty to see between the surface and 5m.

The gently sloping reef boasts excellent hard and soft corals, including black coral shrubs, patches of healthy table corals and clusters of gorgonians at

Location: Southern Strait of Gubal, between Tawila and Shadwan Islands

Depth Range: 5-20m (16-65ft)

Access: Boat or live-aboard

Expertise Rating: Novice

about 15m. This diverse coral habitat hosts the typical bounty of reef fish.

Toward the end of your dive, linger awhile between 10m and the surface. This section of the reef hosts a myriad of colorful species, including sergeants, cornetfish, fusiliers, surgeonfish, bannerfish, lionfish, morays, groupers, triggerfish and bigeyes, to name but a few. Bluespotted stingrays lurk in the sandy patches, and if you're lucky, pelagics may buzz past.

50 Sha'ab el-Erg

Sha'ab el-Erg is a huge horseshoe-shaped reef offering several diving areas. Snorkeling is also popular here, as conditions are usually very safe.

Location: Off El Gouna

Depth Range: 5-15m (16-50ft)

Access: Boat

Expertise Rating: Novice

One of the most popular dive sites is **Dolphin House**, on the southwest side of the reef, named for regular dolphin sightings in the adjacent channel. Here a massive boulder rises up from the seabed at 15m to just below the surface, separated from the main reef by the sandy channel. The typical dive plan is to circumnavigate the boulder at ascending depths.

Rich coral growth coats the boulder, including colorful soft corals, spectacular table corals and other stony species. A cavelet at 7m is packed with glassfish, lionfish and anthias—a must for photographers. You'll find a wide range of colorful reef species, including snappers, groupers and bannerfish, as well as bluespotted stingrays and the occasional turtle. Though there's enough here to keep you happy for a whole dive, you might want to take a look at the main reef—air permitting.

East of the main reef, **Poseidon's Garden** epitomizes the healthy coral garden. At less than 15m, close to the main reef, you'll swim over a field of lush coral formations, including table and brain corals. Clams add a touch of color, together with butterflyfish, angelfish, bannerfish, groupers and parrotfish, as well as clouds of glassfish and anthias flitting around the bigger coral heads. Poseidon's Garden is also a great place for checkout dives.

Also east of the main reef, **Manta Point** comprises a gentle slope. As the name suggests, manta rays sometimes visit the area, especially in February and March. This site is often done as a drift dive.

GAVIN ANDERSON

Divers regularly spot dolphins in the southwest channel.

51 Umm Qamar

A longstanding favorite, Umm Qamar is probably the northernmost site accessible by day boat from Hurghada and the southernmost from El Gouna. It's a long, thin island stretching north-south.

Dive boats usually anchor above a sandy plateau dotted with coral pinnacles in about 12m on the southeast side—an area sheltered from wind and waves. To the east, a steep drop-off plummets into the depths. Swim north along the wall at about 20 to 25m before ascending to about 5 to 10m for your return.

Location: 9km (5.6 miles) north of the Giftun Islands

Depth Range: 10-27m (33-90ft)

Access: Boat

Expertise Rating: Intermediate

Apart from the thrill of diving a drop-off, the highlight of the site is a series of massive boulders bulging from the wall. They act as magnets for small reef species, not to mention eager photographers. The first one is the most scenic. It is peppered with crevices and tunnels that provide sanctuary to groupers and is also festooned with delicate gorgonians and soft corals. Clusters of swift anthias and glassfish flit about the top.

The second boulder is less prolific in marine life, but the third offers a worthwhile cave at its base, the entrance at 27m. While crown-of-thorns sea stars have wreaked havoc on the coral growth, fish life is decent and includes snappers, bigeyes, bannerfish, scorpionfish, sergeants, unicornfish, angelfish, fusiliers and morays hiding in the crevices. Stay in the top 10m, which boasts some nice overhangs. Keep an eye on the blue for passing pelagics.

MARK WEBSTER

Crown-of-thorns sea stars have a voracious appetite for coral.

52 Giftun Islands

Giftun Kebir and Giftun Saghir (Big and Small Giftun) rank among the Red Sea's most popular diving spots. Every day, several dozen diving and snorkeling boats throng to these two jewels resting in clear turquoise waters. Due to their popularity, the islands have been granted protected status, and regulations are strictly enforced. Each diver must pay an entry fee on top of the price of the dive. The entry fees help support Egyptian environmental efforts.

Location: Off Hurghada

Depth Range: 5-30m (16-100ft)

Access: Boat

Expertise Rating: Intermediate

From Hurghada it takes between 45 and 90 minutes to reach the sites. Big Giftun comes first, dwarfing Small Giftun to the southeast. You'll still have to cope with other dive boats, and it can get quite busy underwater at some sites, but the quality and diversity of the diving more than make up for the hassles. Nearly 10 sites are regularly offered, with a variety of dive plans to suit all experience levels. Another big draw is that there are always several sheltered sites, whatever the weather conditions.

Hamda, also known as **Stone Beach**, is one of the most adrenaline-pumping spots. On the east side of Big Giftun, it boasts a steep wall tumbling to 50m and below. Visibility is often excellent, and you'll spot throngs of morays and bigeyes. A couple of sand patches and a plateau at about 20m break the monotony of the wall. Coral growth is excellent and small fish life abundant, especially in the upper sections of the reef. Keep an eye on the blue for barracuda and the occasional turtle or shark.

Another hot spot is **Erg Somaya**, on the east side of Small Giftun. This site features a steep coral slope sprouting two massive pinnacles between 18 and 25m.

Crystal-clear sheltered lagoons draw a daily throng of dive boats to the Giftun Islands.

These spires are alight with shimmering anthias, making them a photographer's delight. Explore the overhangs, caverns and various nooks at about 25m. Healthy hard corals dominate the reef, along with a few soft corals and lush gorgonians jutting from the wall between 25 and 30m. Turtles, rays, fusiliers, goatfish, parrotfish, groupers, snappers, angelfish, morays and schooling trevallies are regulars. Watch for the occasional passing pelagic.

The channel separating the two islands offers several sites to choose from, including **Sha'ab Sabina** and **Erg Sabina**. Sha'ab Sabina is an easy drift dive. You'll hover over a vast field of healthy corals and sand patches in less than 15m, where sandy mini-canyons alternate with coral ridges. Expect to see puffers, snappers, fusiliers, angelfish, butterflyfish, bluespotted stingrays, anemones and the occasional turtle or Napoleonfish. Barren patches of dead coral mark the main reef and the end of your dive. Nearby Erg Sabina is a shallow dive, with numerous coral mounds surrounding a main mound that breaks the surface.

Police Station, also known as **Small Giftun Drift**, is an advanced drift dive on the south side of Small Giftun. You enter within sight of police barracks—hence the name. Keep the reef to your right and swim down a sloping reef to a steeper section that gives way to a sandy plateau at about 20m. Majestic gorgonians stand in regimental rows perpendicular to the drop-off between 25 and 30m. Fish life is abundant, with clouds of anthias, bannerfish, goatfish, fusiliers, snappers, butterflyfish, surgeonfish, groupers, batfish, morays and lionfish, not to mention the occasional pelagic cruising by the wall.

But Wait ... There's More

Other major sites in the El Gouna/Hurghada region:

- **Sha'ab Umm Usk:** One of the northernmost sites in the Strait of Gubal, this is a favorite overnight anchorage for live-aboards. Several dive plans tour the outer slope of this horseshoe-shaped reef.

- **Sha'ab Abu Nigara:** East of El Gouna, this reef in less than 15m (50ft) offers dive plans to suit all levels.

- **Sha'ab Abu Galawa:** Southeast of El Gouna, this reef is ideal for novice divers and underwater photographers.

- **Sha'ab Umm Qamar:** Badly damaged by crown-of-thorns sea stars, this onetime favorite site south of Umm Qamar features a drop-off, the remains of a wreck and numerous cavelets, fissures and overhangs in the shallows. Gorgonians thrive here.

- **Carless (Careless) Reef:** In the open ocean north of the Giftuns, this popular site was also ravaged by crown-of-thorns sea stars. Beside a steep drop-off, two pinnacles rise to the surface from a plateau at about 16m (53ft). Pelagics are common.

- **Sha'ab el-Fanadir:** Just north of Hurghada, this is an easy site, ideal for beginners, courses and checkout dives. Marked by an abundance of fish in shallow water.

- *Excalibur:* Just off Hurghada, this live-aboard caught fire and sank in December 1995. She is 35m (115ft) in length and lies at 22m (72ft).Good checkout wreck dive.

- *El Minija:* Just east of Hurghada naval base, this oceangoing minesweeper sank after being struck starboard by a small bomb. Maximum depth is 30m (100ft).

53 Erg Abu Ramada

Erg Abu Ramada features a row of three imposing coral ergs (pillars) that rise from a sandy plateau at 20m and almost reach the surface. The pillars are connected by saddles and resemble a small mountain range. The typical dive plan consists of swimming around the ergs, starting from the base at about 20m and spiraling to the surface.

Location: Southeast side of Abu Ramada, just south of Small Giftun

Depth Range: 5-20m (16-65ft)

Access: Boat

Expertise Rating: Intermediate

The pinnacle tops literally teem with small fish life. Numerous cavelets, splits, fissures, nooks and crannies provide perfect hiding places for small marine life. The pinnacles also attract Napoleonfish, schooling fusiliers, bigeyes and cornetfish, while rays lie buried in the sand and pelagics sometimes swim by. Coral growth includes gorgonians and multicolored soft corals.

Be aware that weather conditions are a key factor here. The site is exposed to the winds and often experiences tricky currents. A drift dive is an option for experienced divers.

54 Aruk Giftun

A safe and easy dive, Aruk Giftun features a vast expanse of coral mounds rising from a flat, sandy seabed in less than 12m. If it's windy, expect some surface current.

There are actually three sites here: Aruk Giftun, **Aruk Gigi** and **Aruk Diana**. Some mounds are scattered, while others stand in formation. Several reach the surface. There is no set dive plan, other than circling the mounds from the bottom up.

Location: South of Big Giftun

Depth Range: 5-15m (16-50ft)

Access: Boat

Expertise Rating: Novice

The coral heads are crowned with dazzling aggregations of anthias. Also look for snappers, scorpionfish, gobies, nudibranchs, lionfish, groupers, goatfish, fusiliers, butterflyfish, bigeyes, parrotfish, angelfish, pipefish, triggerfish, cardinalfish, bluespotted stingrays and small morays. Coral growth, primarily hard species, is varied and healthy.

This site is a bonanza for photographers. The white sandy floor reflects the sunlight, transforming the whole area into a vivid natural studio.

Pyjama nudibranchs grow to 4.5cm (1.8 inches).

55 Gota Abu Ramada

Just south of Abu Ramada, Gota Abu Ramada is also known as **The Aquarium** due to the mind-boggling abundance of marine life on display, especially smaller species. The site is a paradise for photographers, as well as a popular choice for night dives and a great snorkeling spot. As a result, it's often a bit crowded.

The site comprises two impressive pinnacles on a flat sandy seafloor in less than 15m, just off a main reef. The pinnacles support an array of multicolored species, including angelfish, butterfly-

Location: 5km (3.1 miles) south of the Giftun Islands

Depth Range: 3-15m (10-49ft)

Access: Boat

Expertise Rating: Novice

fish, parrotfish and bigeyes. Trevallies and snappers are also common. Explore the numerous smaller pinnacles along the seafloor, but pay attention to the current.

From here swim to a lush hard-coral garden east of the main reef, which boasts clusters of dome-shaped brain corals at about 10m. Schools of bannerfish and butterflyfish, goatfish, big snappers and bigeyes make the scene, as well as shoaling sweetlips.

Turn back till you reach the mooring line, then head to the upper part of the reef, in about 5m, where myriad swirling damselfish add a touch of color and action.

Look beneath Gota Abu Ramada's protective overhangs to find shoals of blackspotted sweetlips.

GAVIN ANDERSON

56 Ras Disha

Just north of Abu Hashish, Ras Disha boasts a beautiful setting, in turquoise waters with the mountains as a backdrop.

Location: South of Hurghada

Depth Range: 5-15m (16-50ft)

Access: Boat

Expertise Rating: Novice

Here several large coral heads stud a sandy floor off a main reef. In less than 12m, the coral heads are alive with a pleasing array of colorful reef species, including lionfish, morays, puffers, snappers, groupers, nudibranchs, soldierfish, bannerfish and anthias, among others. Add to the list the usual sand-dwellers and predators like barracuda, and you'll have a fair idea of the action. It's also a good area to look for seamoths.

Beyond the coral heads is a patch of seagrass and an attractive coral garden at

about 15m, a nice spot for photographers. Stony corals predominate, along with a few healthy soft-coral thickets.

Finish your dive on the pinnacle beneath the mooring. It features a scenic arch at 7m with a billowing curtain of glassfish and anthias. Spend your safety stop honing your photographic skills.

57 Abu Hashish

Abu Hashish combines attractive topography with varied marine life, all at depths of less than 15m. The dive boat moors in a protected lagoon about 5m deep. Leave the lagoon through a small canyon that scars the reef tongue. The canyon is filled with storm-damaged table corals.

Location: South of Hurghada

Depth Range: 5-15m (16-50ft)

Access: Boat

Expertise Rating: Novice

It opens onto a gently sloping sandy plateau strewn with coral boulders. Take time to explore the most attractive ones, richly adorned with soft corals and riddled with intricate nooks. Octopuses, rays, barracuda, morays and groupers are common on the plateau.

Return to the reef and follow it in either direction, hovering between 5 and 10m. It features pristine soft and hard corals and prolific marine life. Finish your dive back in the lagoon. If the north-south current is too strong, a drift dive along the reef is an option.

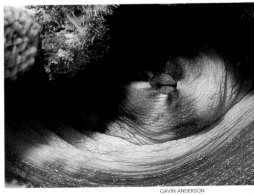

GAVIN ANDERSON

An octopus peers from hiding with one red eye.

Safaga

For the most part, Safaga defies the hordes—though that is rapidly changing. Somehow it had been overlooked as divers charged headlong to Egypt's southern Red Sea coast, desperate to sink their teeth into some virgin reefs.

Tucked as it is just to the south of Hurghada, few would consider the potential of this little bay with its moderate dive fleet and, perhaps more important, limited nightlife. But its charm is undeniable, and the nightlife will improve over time.

GAVIN ANDERSON

Don't let the donkey throw you—laid-back Safaga has several professionally run dive centers.

Safaga Dive Sites

	Good Snorkeling	Novice	Intermediate	Advanced
58 Ras Umm Hesiwa & Sha'ab Saiman	●		●	
59 Ras Abu Soma			●	
60 The Tobias	●	●		
61 Gamul Soghira & Gamul Kebira	●	●		
62 Panorama Reef			●	
63 Middle Reef	●		●	
64 Abu Kafan			●	
65 Sha'ab Sheer	●	●		
66 Salem Express			●	
67 Sha'ab Humdallah		●		

Safaga, however, is a well-established resort for German and Scandinavian divers. Many of the centers are staffed by Germans. This is largely a good thing, for although they are laid-back and relaxed, they are also well organized. The airfills are always clean, the boats leave when they should, the food aboard is generally excellent and the professionalism of the instructors and guides is mostly second to none.

As the shoreline reefs are poor, most of the diving is done by day boat. The outer reefs see a steady stream of live-aboards, which stop off on their way back to Hurghada. The level of diving varies immensely, from easy and sheltered inner reefs like Tobia Arba'a to the exposed deep walls of Abu Kafan.

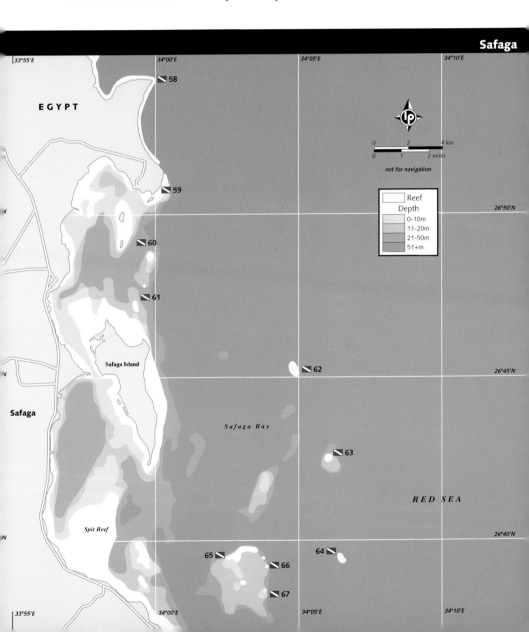

Safaga

58 Ras Umm Hesiwa & Sha'ab Saiman

Location: 10km (6.2 miles) north of Safaga

Depth Range: 3-30m (10-100ft)

Access: Boat

Expertise Rating: Intermediate

As you round the point at Ras Umm Hesiwa, the current hits you like a slap in the face. If you have the air and the determination, you can continue down a long tongue of reef that juts rudely seaward. Divers have encountered thresher sharks deep on this point.

In the lee of the headland is a more mellow kind of dive. Huge table corals line the plateau, which local guides will tell you often shelter whitetip reef sharks. Whether you believe them or not is a different matter. The site is fairly exposed to the elements and is only accessible in the best conditions. Generally the wind calms slightly in the afternoon, opening the door to an even better site around the corner.

Sha'ab Saiman is a little-known coral ridge running parallel to the shore reef just a few hundred yards past Ras Umm Hesiwa. Separating this reef from the shore is a narrow sandy canyon, 8m at its shallowest point and sloping off in either direction. The ridge also slopes away on either side. Shoals of snappers and chub hang out in the shallow water, while barracuda, jacks and batfish dominate the plateau on the seaward side.

59 Ras Abu Soma

Location: 5km (3.1 miles) north of Safaga

Depth Range: 3-30m (10-100ft)

Access: Boat

Expertise Rating: Intermediate

Diving Ras Abu Soma is something of a game of roulette. If luck is on your side, you'll be diving with barracuda, jacks, snappers, batfish and surgeonfish. The big boys sighted here have included guitar sharks, leopard sharks, stingrays, eagle rays and hammerheads, as well as manta rays in March and April. If luck isn't on your side, you won't see much more than the odd boxfish.

The ras (headland) here is the one that defines the northern limits of Safaga Bay. The dive is usually done as a drift, jumping in beyond the headland but well before the beacon. Beneath is a steep wall and lots of blue water.

Heading south, you'll find a ledge, which soon turns into a broad plateau. On the lip of this plateau at about 35m is a cave, teeming with glassfish and dripping with soft corals and sponges. You can while away a few minutes in here, closely watched by a large grouper that guards its entrance.

Moving back up takes you across the plateau and past some large, prehistoric-looking table corals, then up to the shallows, where you finish your dive.

60 The Tobias

The reefs known collectively as the Tobias vary widely in quality. **Tobia Arba'a** comprises a group of closely packed ergs. Though *arba'a* means four, there are actually seven of them, hence their other name, **The Seven Pinnacles**. The colors here are stunning, but the site tends to get overcrowded, especially when the weather prevents diving on the outer reefs.

Location: North Safaga Bay

Depth Range: 5-18m (16-60ft)

Access: Boat

Expertise Rating: Novice

Tobia Hamra and **Tobia Kebira** are generally less interesting than the others, though they offer the best option for novices.

This leaves **Tobia Soghira**, a Y-shaped group of coral mushrooms—at least, the arrangement looks Y-shaped from the surface. Once underwater, however, their grouping is seemingly random, and they pose a navigational nightmare for the average diver armed with anything less than a submersible GPS. With a wide array of canyons, tunnels and swim-throughs, it is easy to forget about the burdensome task of not getting lost and surrender yourself to simply having fun. Bluespotted stingrays, trig-gerfish, surgeonfish and emperors all have their place on this reef.

The seven pinnacles at Tobia Arba'a are ablaze with colorful life.

GAVIN ANDERSON

61 Gamul Soghira & Gamul Kebira

This set of shallow inshore reefs is your best bet for quality diving if the weather turns nasty, but that's not to say it's a last resort.

Gamul Kebira is a donut-shaped reef with a number of outlying ergs, just to the north of Safaga Island. To the south is a long, thin and nondescript reef, and all around are seagrass beds. The best dive plan is to drop in around the ergs north of the donut-shaped reef and then swim back to the boat moored in the shelter of the inner lagoon. A school of sinister-looking barracuda sometimes patrols the ergs, and eagle rays cruise by from time to time. The seabed is home to a colony of garden eels and occasional seamoths.

Location: North Safaga Bay

Depth Range: 3-15m (10-50ft)

Access: Boat

Expertise Rating: Novice

Gamul Soghira lies slightly to the north. It's a round reef with four outlying ergs, only two of which can be seen from the surface. All the ergs are stunning, but the best is the southernmost one, which is often swathed down one side in a shoal of glassfish and silversides, with the normal predators in attendance.

62 Panorama Reef

Down the outer edge of Safaga Bay runs a line of offshore reefs, much like the buoys marking the swimming area of a beach—Panorama is the northern-

Location: Outer Safaga Bay

Depth Range: 3-40m (10-130ft)

Access: Boat or live-aboard

Expertise Rating: Intermediate

most of these. It also goes by the Arabic name **Abu Alama**, meaning "Father of the Mast"—a reference to the concrete pillar at the north point, which once served the role now played by an automated beacon.

The reef is oval, its walls tumbling steeply down to a ledge that slopes from 12 to about 25m before plunging into the abyss. The ledge on the west side is wider, sandier and generally more interesting than that on the outer, east side.

GAVIN ANDERSON

Bigeye trevallies circle above the reef.

The journey by day boat from Safaga takes between 60 and 90 minutes. As the boat must take the northerly sea on the beam, it can get quite uncomfortable. Once it's moored, there is plenty of protection. Live-aboards are equally well protected, although an overnight stay depends largely on the skipper's nerve.

With often-raging currents prevailing from the north, the dive is best done as a drift. Starting on the north plateau, work your way down to its northernmost point for the best sightings of trevallies, as well as schooling barracuda and unicornfish. Past sightings have included numerous dolphins, eagle rays, grey reef sharks, silvertips and even oceanic whitetip sharks—though as the reef has grown in popularity, such sightings have become less common.

Divers should turn with the current and head south with air to spare. Drifting along either side of the reef, you may spot crocodilefish, scorpionfish, turtles and Napoleonfish. Also look for a colony of some 50 to 60 anemones.

Where to Find Sharks

While the southern Red Sea is better known for shark encounters, these awesome predators frequent the entire sea. Following is a list of shark species that roam the region and where each is commonly spotted. For more information see "Red Sea Shark Primer," page 161.

Leopard sharks—Shallow sandy reefs in the Gulf of Suez and off Safaga

Nurse sharks—Shallow rocky reefs in Yemen, Eritrea and Djibouti

Whitetip reef sharks—Anywhere and everywhere

Blacktip reef sharks—Coastal lagoons and reefs in the Deep South, Sudan, Eritrea and Yemen

Grey reef sharks—Jackson Reef in the Strait of Tiran, Ras Mohammed (in winter) and current-swept offshore reefs in the Deep South and Sudan

Silvertip sharks—Typically on current-swept plateaus in Sudan; occasionally off Safaga and on offshore reefs in the Deep South

Silky sharks—Surface waters of Sha'ab Rumi in Sudan

Oceanic whitetip sharks—Surface waters around Ras Mohammed, The Brothers, Elphinstone Reef and in Sudan

Thresher sharks—Jackson Reef, Small Brother, Daedalus Reef and offshore reefs in the Deep South

Hammerhead sharks—North side of Jackson Reef, Ras Mohammed (in early morning), Abu Kafan in Safaga, Elphinstone Reef, The Brothers, Daedalus Reef and in Sudan

Whale sharks—Gulf of Aqaba, offshore islands in the Deep South, Bab el-Mandeb Strait

GAVIN PARSONS

63 Middle Reef

Middle Reef might not be as dizzyingly steep as its neighbors, but it makes up for this with colorful and dramatic hard-coral gardens, which are rated by some as the best in Egypt.

The better dive is on the east reef, which slopes gradually down to a field of brain corals, lunar in appearance. A series of sandy gullies and yet more brain corals takes you slowly down toward a drop-off at the northeast, which in normal current conditions (usually strong and in your face) takes about 30 minutes.

Currents prevail from the north, so if drift diving is an option, the north end is where to jump in. Cruise back along either side of the reef, but take care not to get lost. Because the reef is so large and featureless, it's easy to get carried away and end up surfacing down-current from your boat. The current would usually prevent you from finning back, leaving you floating into oblivion, praying you'll be noticed.

The plateau to the southeast of the reef never really drops off. Instead, it

Location: Outer Safaga Bay

Depth Range: 3-30m (10-100ft)

Access: Boat or live-aboard

Expertise Rating: Intermediate

stretches a full 500m to a ridge of habilis (pinnacles) known as **Hal-Hal**. Hal-Hal is a fisherman's term meaning restless sea, and it's easy to see how this site got its name. There is no physical protection for boats, as the habilis stop 3m short of the surface—if anything, they jack up the waves, making surface conditions worse. Nine times out of ten the spot is undiveable.

Choppy it may be, but it's still worth-while. The site is compact, but chock-full of life and ablaze with soft corals and gorgonians. Often the currents are so strong that the anthias cling to the slopes for protection, drawing groupers from their caves for the chance at an easy meal.

64 Abu Kafan

"The Deep One"—that's the meaning, more or less, of Abu Kafan. Cruising over the northern plateau, you'd be left wondering why. Shallow sunlit sand patches are interspersed with coral outcrops, and down the center a ridge of towers reaches toward the surface. The often-raging current ensures luxuriant soft-coral growth.

It's as you turn to leave the plateau that you realize the relevance of this reef's name. Sheer walls plummet headlong toward the seafloor, hundreds of meters below. It's a mellow drift from

Location: Outer Safaga Bay

Depth Range: 3-40m (10-130ft)

Access: Boat or live-aboard

Expertise Rating: Intermediate

here to the south point, past walls of overhangs draped with gorgonians and black corals. At the south end is a solitary erg that marks the end of your dive.

The plateau is a good place to spot glasseyes schooling en masse. They hover just above the reef, and if a big predator or perhaps a diver happens by, they rush to the coral for cover. Turtles and barracuda share the shallow slopes, the barracuda every so often schooling in the hundreds.

Abu Kafan lies 90 to 120 minutes southeast of Safaga, a daytrip by boat. The upside is that live-aboards, which can moor overnight at nearby Sha'ab Sheer, have a monopoly on early-morning diving but are often gone by the time day boats arrive.

Abu Kafan's prolific slopes support fish life ranging from tiny anthias to huge lyretail groupers.

65 Sha'ab Sheer

The brain coral garden at Sha'ab Sheer looks like a giant sheet of bubble wrap, or perhaps a field of tightly packed mushrooms. These huge monoliths of color burst from a seabed at about 12m, painting the seascape green, blue and beige.

Sha'ab Sheer itself is a horseshoe of reef more than a kilometer long. On its east end, two satellite reefs and a couple of ergs stand about 10m away from the reef proper, and it's in the channel between that the brain coral garden lies. It can either be dived as a drift, starting on the reef's outer slopes and following the current back into the lagoon, or it can be dived from a boat moored south of the channel.

Location: South Safaga Bay

Depth Range: 3-15m (10-50ft)

Access: Boat or live-aboard

Expertise Rating: Novice

While the corals dazzle, fish life is just average. Bannerfish, redtooth triggerfish and trevallies reside on the outer slopes, and schools of tuna or mackerel occasionally charge through. Bicolor parrotfish, slingjaw wrasses and scribbled filefish add a splash of color. Explore the gullies to find all species of triggerfish.

66 *Salem Express*

The *Salem Express* has been described by some as one of the best wreck dives in the Red Sea, though that opinion clearly demonstrates either ignorance or callous disregard of the ship's tragic story. The Egyptian ferry struck the nearby reef close to midnight on December 15, 1991, and sank within minutes.

Location: South Safaga Bay

Depth Range: 15-30m (50-100ft)

Access: Boat or live-aboard

Expertise Rating: Intermediate

Without going into explicit details of how hundreds of pilgrims returning from Mecca met their end, or the way in which any form of rescue operation failed to materialize, suffice it to say the dive should be one of reflection rather than enjoyment. And before you decide whether to visit this steel coffin or not, make sure to ask some of the older locals what happened that night. Most of the suitcases, clothes and duty-free packages that once littered the wreck have now drifted away, but the place retains its sobering atmosphere. Its unused lifeboats lie side by side on the seafloor.

The most useful advice is to take a look, spare a thought for the victims and then head to the nearby reefs. Spend your time savoring the beauty of the shallow waters and simply relishing this fragile life that we all too often take for granted.

Lifeboats remain in place beneath their davits—sobering reminders of the souls lost.

GAVIN ANDERSON

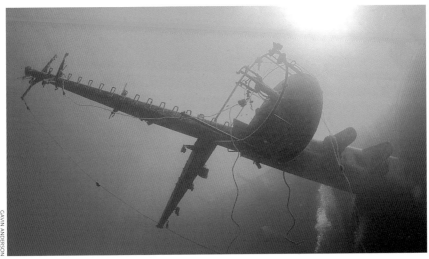

At rest in 30m (100ft) on her starboard side, the *Salem Express* is a stunning yet mournful sight.

67 Sha'ab Humdallah

Location: South Safaga Bay

Depth Range: 5-18m (16-60ft)

Access: Boat or live-aboard

Expertise Rating: Novice

Two hours by day boat may seem like a lot of hassle to go through just to dive a small bunch of pinnacles sitting atop a sand patch. But these pinnacles are everything the Red Sea is about.

As Red Sea pinnacles go, they are fairly tall, rising from the seafloor at 15 to 18m. They are arranged much like the five on dice, with the smallest but perhaps most beautiful pillar at the center. A tunnel lined in soft corals runs through the middle of the northernmost pillar, sheltering several pale-colored greasy groupers, while the westernmost pillar is split in two. Look atop the surrounding sandy seafloor for numerous cone shells, but don't touch.

The site is on the south end of the Sha'ab Sheer plateau and, therefore, makes an excellent second dive after a morning at the nearby wreck of the *Salem Express* or at Abu Kafan to the east. Like Hal-Hal at Middle Reef, these pinnacles offer little protection from the weather.

Several greasy groupers have claimed a tunnel.

Quseir

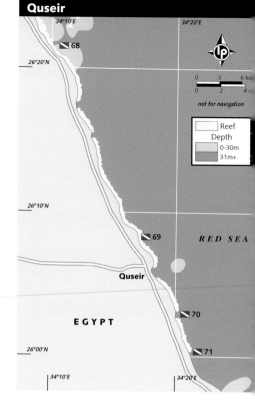

For centuries Quseir was one of the Red Sea's most important trade and export hubs and a major exit point for pilgrims traveling to Mecca. The opening of the Suez Canal in 1869 put an end to the port's former prosperity.

Today sleepy Quseir holds a charm absent from Egypt's other Red Sea towns. Tourist development has not quite reached this far south (Quseir is 85km (53 miles) south of Safaga), and you'll appreciate its laid-back atmosphere.

About 10 sites are regularly dived in the area, to the north and south of Quseir. All are shore dives, best accessed by four-wheel-drive vehicle, though sometimes by boat. The region offers varied topography, abundant marine life and several excellent house reefs. Another draw is the absence of crowds on the sites—though that soon may change.

Be aware that prevailing winds determine dive conditions here. Wind-driven waves can complicate your entry, and you may have to cope with heavy surf and runoff.

Transport to Quseir's nearshore sites is via four-wheel-drive vehicle.

Quseir Dive Sites

	Good Snorkeling	Novice	Intermediate	Advanced
68 Maklouf			●	
69 El Qadim (Sirena Beach House Reef)	●		●	
70 El Kaf		●		
71 Soug Bohar (Kilo 15 South)			●	

68 Maklouf

Maklouf begins with a shore entry through a winding canyon in the reeftop. The canyon opens onto a sloping sandy area studded with a jumble of huge coral towers interspersed with sand gullies and ravines at various depths. These coral blocks loom darkly from the seafloor, and you'll feel like you're wending your way through a medieval castle.

Follow the sandy trails and work your way up and around the towers, between 10 and 25m. The coral structures are carved with fissures and overhangs that shelter a variety of reef species, including fusiliers, damselfish, bannerfish, puffers, groupers, lionfish, bluespotted stingrays and the odd phosphorescent anemone.

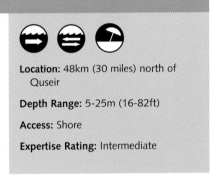

Location: 48km (30 miles) north of Quseir

Depth Range: 5-25m (16-82ft)

Access: Shore

Expertise Rating: Intermediate

Leave the towers and swim south to a plateau at about 25m, where healthy table corals straddle the sand. Keep an eye on the blue for passing mackerel, tuna, turtles and sharks.

Currents and runoff can make your return through the canyon tricky. When it's windy, this site is not recommended.

69 El Qadim (Sirena Beach House Reef)

El Qadim is in a small bay abutted by Sirena Beach and the Mövenpick Resort. Though it's a house reef—more or less exclusive to the hotel's resident dive center—sunbathing guests seem largely oblivious to the marvels just offshore. El Qadim is a splendid natural photographic studio, a great spot for both macro and wide-angle shots. It suits all levels of

Location: 7km (4.3 miles) north of Quseir

Depth Range: 5-30m (16-100ft)

Access: Shore

Expertise Rating: Intermediate

divers and offers good conditions, even in bad weather.

Both sides of the bay are worth a look, and several dive plans are possible. Most divers enter the bay from the Subex dive center pontoon and meander to the south side. The middle of the bay is sandy and dotted with coral pinnacles at 15 to 25m, a playground for small species. You'll also find the usual sand-dwelling fauna, including goatfish, bluespotted stingrays,

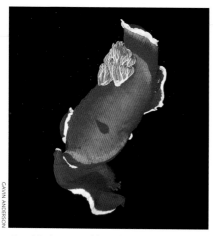

Spanish dancer nudibranchs perform at night.

crocodilefish, flounder, garden eels and seamoths. The south side is rather steep and drops down to 40m at the mouth of the bay.

Linger a while at a section boasting a network of interesting canyons. The usual species of multicolored reef fish flutter about, and observant divers will also spot nudibranchs, which are fine macrophotography subjects. Look also for pipefish, lionfish and scorpionfish.

Beyond the canyons is an elaborate system of interconnected caves at 4 to 7m. Sunbeams play through skylights in the caves, while soldierfish hang out in the dark corners. Photographers will be able to take some good silhouette shots. Though the caves are relatively safe and well lit, novice divers should not enter without a guide.

Other dive plans include exploring the north side of the bay and the seaward edges, where there is a good chance at spotting pelagics. The bay is also a great site for courses and a superb spot for night dives, when lobsters and Spanish dancers make their appearance.

70 El Kaf

El Kaf is an easy dive that suits all levels of divers, as well as photographers. Its calm waters attract local dive centers when the prevailing northerlies are blowing. Shore entry is easy, as divers don't have to walk across the reeftop. Runoff is easy to manage.

A wide sandy basin leads to a canyon pitted with small caves and passages along the wall to your right—best explored during your safety stop at the end of the dive. Look for barracuda near the canyon entrance. Follow the canyon to a coral slope at the reef edge.

Location: 10km (6.2 miles) south of Quseir

Depth Range: 18-25m (60-82ft)

Access: Shore

Expertise Rating: Novice

The labyrinthine topography is spectacular, featuring numerous massive coral boulders scattered on a sandy floor beside a drop-off. The reef here is incredibly

Underwater Photography

The Red Sea offers tremendous opportunities for underwater photography. As on land, taking good pictures underwater depends on lighting, composition and a healthy dose of luck. Following are some tips to get you started:

First, watch out for air conditioning in hotel rooms or even live-aboard cabins. Both your underwater and land camera will fog up when taken outside and may need up to 30 minutes to acclimatize.

Colors fade quickly at depth, so you'll need to use a flash or strobe. The key is to balance the light from your strobe with the available sunlight. If you're taking macro or close-up pictures, use your strobe in TTL mode, but work in manual mode for wide-angle shots. (When aimed at the sun, the Nikonos V and other underwater cameras can be fooled into thinking there is plenty of light; strobes set in TTL mode will hold back and not fire sufficiently.)

Estimate how far your subject is from the camera and adjust the strobe's power setting accordingly. Remember, your strobe will only be really effective for up to 2m (6ft). You'll want to get in close to your subject and use the widest-angle lens you can. Good options include the 15mm Nikonos lens or a 20mm housed lens.

To lend your pictures impact, shoot toward the sun, lighting the subject with your strobes. This will give the impression that the sun is lighting your subject, not your strobe. For rich blue backgrounds, meter into the blue away from the sun, using either your camera's built-in meter or a handheld meter.

Don't forget to try some natural light pictures. Wrecks, big shoals of fish, turtles, dolphins and sharks all make compelling subjects for silhouettes. Switch off your strobes and use a slightly faster shutter speed, but remember to meter the ambient light for a nice blue background.

To ensure your photographs are properly exposed, bracket, taking two or three shots of the same subject at different exposure settings. In poor visibility, get close to your subject and hand-hold your strobe as far from the camera as possible to limit backscatter from light hitting plankton and other floating matter.

Patterns, ovals, leading lines, triangles and curves all make for interesting composition. Avoid distracting mergers such as a fish's tail coming out of another fish's head, and give your subjects somewhere to swim. Use fellow divers to add perspective to the scene.

Finally, rinse your camera in fresh water after every dive and once more at the end of the day. A soak for 30 minutes or so is helpful to loosen any stubborn salt crystals. And remember to bring your own tool kit, with grease, batteries, tissues, jeweler's screwdrivers and anything else you may need to do a quick fix.

GAVIN ANDERSON

varied, with sandy ravines, overhangs, canyons, pinnacles, cavelets and swim-throughs, all at depths less than 25m.

GAVIN ANDERSON

Emperor angelfish are drawn to El Kaf's healthy corals.

Go to your planned depth and work your way up and around the complex of structures. Heading back to the canyon entrance, spend some time in a cavern at 8m, which is packed with fish, then in a scenic small amphitheater carved into the reef at about 6m.

Though a storm damaged the coral in 1996, its growth remains fairly healthy. As for fish life, you'll find a good variety of reef species. Unicornfish, Indian Ocean bird wrasses, groupers, schools of fusiliers, butterflyfish, triggerfish, glassfish and puffers abound. Look amid the sand for gobies, goatfish, flounder and snake eels, and keep an eye on the blue for whitetip reef sharks, turtles and Napoleonfish.

71 Soug Bohar (Kilo 15 South)

Soug Bohar boasts a varied seascape of reefs, channels, pinnacles and cavelets. The dive begins with a shore entry into a curved channel carved into the reeftop at about 5m. This channel opens onto a moderately sloping reef.

Facing the channel and detached from the main reef, a huge contoured pinnacle rises from the seafloor, topped with a host of small, colorful species. Divers usually swim to the right (south), where the reef curves shoreward into a scenic bay highlighted by a series of big boulders.

Continue south between 10 and 25m and you'll enter a range of mountainlike coral boulders laced with sand valleys and gullies. The area shelters an underwater Eden of lush coral growth and abundant fish life. Look for lionfish, scorpionfish, surgeonfish, puffers, snap-

Location: 15km (9.3 miles) south of Quseir

Depth Range: 4-25m (13-82ft)

Access: Shore

Expertise Rating: Intermediate

pers, bluespotted stingrays, pipefish and fusiliers, among others. If you're lucky, you may spot whitetips, eagle rays or even a guitar shark.

Return along the main reef at about 10m to the main channel near the entry point to explore several cavelets carved into the channel wall. Air permitting, you can explore a second channel next to the main one. Look for nudibranchs in both channels.

Deep South

Egypt's southern Red Sea coast—known locally as the Deep South—begins roughly near the ancient trading town of Quseir. Despite harsh surroundings, Egyptians were mining copper here as early as 4,000 years ago. Now the coast is famed as one of the world's last diving frontiers. Between Quseir and the Sudanese border are some 300km (185 miles) of shoreline, boasting breathtaking dive sites that offer several shipwrecks and encounters with sharks, dolphins and schooling pelagics.

A healthy fringing reef runs nearly the entire length of the coast, dotted with turquoise bays. The colorful seascape contrasts sharply with the monochromatic landscape. Several wadis (dry stream beds) wind down to the sea from the dusty Red Sea Mountains, which top 2,000m (6,550ft).

While this shoreline remains largely unspoiled, tourism is spreading south at an alarming rate. Developers and big hotel chains have bought up much of the coastal land from Quseir to the Sudanese border. Several dive resorts have already opened near Quseir and to the south at Marsa Alam, where a new airport is planned.

This development poses a runoff threat to inshore reefs. And because there aren't nearly enough natural breaks in the fringing reef, developers may want to blast channels through the corals. Whether they are allowed to, only time will tell.

The outlook isn't all bleak. Small coastal plots have been purchased by Red Sea Diving Safari, an environmentally responsible company that operates tented camps, which have little impact on shoreline habitats.

While there are plenty of good sites along the coast, the best diving is found farther offshore. The outer reef systems of Fury Shoal, just north of Ras Banas, and St. John's Reef, some 16km (10 miles) north of the Sudanese border, are especially inviting. Here divers can explore remote pinnacles, spectacular drop-offs and coral-encrusted shipwrecks, some only recently discovered.

Advanced divers flock to four remote islands: The Brothers, 58km (36 miles) northeast of Quseir; Daedalus, 90km (56 miles) east of Marsa Alam; and Rocky and Zabargad, well offshore a few kilometers north of the Sudanese border. The best way to explore the area is by live-aboard. Most live-aboards depart from Hurghada and make either one- or two-week trips south, offering a variety of itineraries.

GAVIN ANDERSON

Tented camps offer divers a low-impact alternative to resorts.

Marsa Galeb to Wadi Gamal

Between Marsa Galeb and Wadi Gamal lie many great dive sites—from Elphinstone Reef and Sha'ab Sharm, where sharks gather, to Sha'ab Samadai, where a family of spinner dolphins hangs out. Diving along the shore is good, though some sites have been damaged by crown-of-thorns sea stars. Several sheltered bays offer diving when conditions deteriorate.

The preferred way to access the area is by live-aboard, though land-based operators have become increasingly popular and now offer a range of options. Most live-aboards leave from Quseir, while divers staying onshore head for Marsa Alam. The town affords easy access to Marsa Abu Dabbab, Sha'ab Marsa Alam, Sha'ab Samadai and Elphinstone Reef. Accommodations are available to suit all budgets, from luxury hotels to small chalets and tented camps.

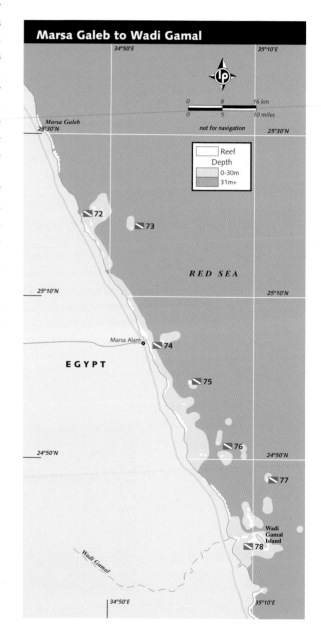

Marsa Galeb to Wadi Gamal Dive Sites

	Good Snorkeling	Novice	Intermediate	Advanced
72 Marsa Abu Dabbab	●		●	
73 Elphinstone Reef				●
74 Sha'ab Marsa Alam & Erg Marsa Alam	●		●	
75 Sha'ab Samadai	●	●		
76 Radir East	●		●	
77 Sha'ab Sharm				●
78 Sha'ab Shirinat	●		●	

72 | Marsa Abu Dabbab

A few adjacent reefs stretch several kilometers offshore from this harbor, comprising a variety of dive sites, from shallow bays with fringing reefs to shallow offshore reefs and solitary ergs. Some of the reefs were damaged by crown-of-thorns sea stars in the late 1990s, though there are signs of recovery.

The largest outer reef is dived most often, as it offers sheltered moorings. Boats usually anchor in sand on the south side. Divers drop in and drift around the north tip, where a coral finger joins another reef at about 10m. There is often some current, so make sure to get your bearings and head in the right direction.

Where you enter, a bank of coral towers climbs steeply from a sandy bottom at 16m. Look within the area's many canyons and swim-throughs for shoals of snappers, sweetlips, unicornfish and occasionally barracuda and

Location: 30km (19 miles) south of Marsa Galeb

Depth Range: 10-16m (33-53ft)

Access: Boat or live-aboard

Expertise Rating: Intermediate

Adult bluespine unicornfish are unmistakable.

whitetip reef sharks. Also keep an eye out for free-swimming moray eels.

The current may be quite strong at the north tip. Taking care to keep some air in reserve, kick hard to round the point. Beyond it the current will shift, and you'll be able to drift effortlessly back to the boat.

73 Elphinstone Reef

Finger-like Elphinstone Reef extends some 300m in length and is one of the best dive sites in the south. Its spectacular walls plunge vertically on both sides to more than 100m and are covered in beautiful soft corals. Fish life includes millions of shoaling anthias, Napoleonfish, large tuna, rabbitfish and schools of jacks and black-and-white snappers.

Location: 12km (7 miles) east of Marsa Abu Dabbab

Depth Range: 20-40m (65-130ft)

Access: Boat or live-aboard

Expertise Rating: Advanced

Shelving plateaus bookend the reef. The south plateau features a garden of soft corals, gorgonians and long curvy sea whips between 20 and 40m. Also keep an eye out for thresher sharks. Don't be tempted to visit the spectacular archway below you—it's between 50 and 60m, below the sport-diving limit.

Draped in colorful soft corals, the north plateau drops in stages from 8 to 25m, then to 40m. Be aware that the current is often very strong, especially at the point. When conditions are right, whitetip and grey reef sharks visit the site. If you're really lucky, hammerheads and the occasional oceanic whitetip might cruise through.

GAVIN ANDERSON

Watch for strong down-currents on this spectacular wall dive.

74 Sha'ab Marsa Alam & Erg Marsa Alam

This kidney-shaped reef offers ample anchorage for boats inside a sheltered lagoon. Diving takes place on the north and south ends of the reef, where mountainous coral blocks loom over sand patches.

The south end slopes gradually down from about 5m to between 25 and 28m. Expect to see shoals of bannerfish, goatfish and butterflyfish as you cruise over the range of coral mountains. Also look for groupers, which visit their favorite cleaning stations. On the northeast side of the reef is a colony of garden eels.

When a current is running, you may have to swim against it for the first five or 10 minutes. Watch for tuna, barracuda and giant trevallies as you cruise along the lip of a drop-off that starts at 30m. You may even see whitetip and blacktip reef sharks.

Erg Marsa Alam is some 500m southeast of Sha'ab Marsa Alam. Festooned with stunning soft corals, the pinnacle makes for great wide-angle

Location: Just east of Marsa Alam

Depth Range: 5-30m (16-100ft)

Access: Boat or live-aboard

Expertise Rating: Intermediate

pictures. This site can only be dived in calm weather.

GAVIN ANDERSON

Jewel-like chromis dart across the coral heads.

75 Sha'ab Samadai

This large, horseshoe-shaped reef offers plenty of shelter for boats, which often overnight in the lagoon on their way south. A pod of up to 60 spinner dolphins also frequents the lagoon, lending it the nickname "Dolphin Reef." The dolphins are curious and friendly, and it's possible to snorkel with them, although they won't necessarily hang around.

Diving typically takes place amid a series of ergs between 10 and 15m on the southwest tip of the main reef. Many of the ergs are interconnected, forming a

Location: 5km (3 miles) offshore, southeast of Marsa Alam

Depth Range: 10-15m (33-50ft)

Access: Boat or live-aboard

Expertise Rating: Novice

network of caves and tunnels. The afternoon sun filters down through cracks and crevices overhead, reflecting off the sandy seafloor. As there are many openings on both sides of the reef, it's possible to lose your sense of direction while inside the caves. Remember that the shallower water lies to the east.

Look amid the site's many caves, coral blocks and sand and seagrass patches to find moray eels, leopard groupers, fusiliers, goatfish and masked butterfly-fish, along with anemonefish, lionfish, gobies and blind shrimp.

Anemonefish top many divers' must-see lists.

You Watch My Back ...

Blind shrimp and gobies are fascinating to watch. They live in symbiosis in holes in the sand. The shrimp keeps the burrow clear of rubble, while the goby stands guard at the entrance, watching for predators. When danger threatens, such as an approaching diver, the goby waves its tail against the shrimp's feelers, warning it to prepare to retreat. If the predator closes in, the goby fans its tail vigorously, chasing the shrimp down the hole, then darting down behind it.

76 Radir East

Tightly grouped ergs wreathed in hard and soft corals reach from a sandy slope at 20m to within 3 or 4m of the surface. The slope falls from 20 to 35m, then trails off to 40m before tumbling over a wall.

Divers usually drop in beside the northernmost erg and drift back to the boat, winding in and out of the ergs. Explore the many overhangs, caves and passages to find Red Sea coralgroupers, turtles and whitetip reef sharks.

This is an exciting dive when a current is running. As you drift along the outside of the ergs, keep an eye out for stingrays and big pelagics. Also watch the blue for passing schools of tuna, jacks or rainbow runners.

Location: 20km (12 miles) south of Sha'ab Samadai

Depth Range: 20-35m (65-115ft)

Access: Live-aboard

Expertise Rating: Intermediate

Around the ergs themselves you'll spot snappers, bannerfish and angel-fish, as well as thousands of brightly colored anthias feeding on plankton brought in by the strong currents. You'll likely be mobbed by shoals of fusiliers and snappers.

Due to the exposed nature of Radir East, calm weather is essential for diving. If conditions deteriorate, there are less dramatic, sheltered sites in the same reef system, including **Radir North** and **Radir el-Bar**.

GAVIN ANDERSON

Radir East features a labyrinth of current-swept channels, overhangs and caves.

77 Sha'ab Sharm

Sha'ab Sharm is a large, kidney-shaped reef atop a huge undersea mountain, thought to be an ancient volcano. Surrounded by sheer walls, with shallow plateaus on either end, it's an impressive dive site. When conditions are right, pelagic and shark sightings are common.

Most dives take place on the southeast plateau, which drops gradually from 15 to 30m before vanishing into the deep. Divers typically drop in on the north side and drift with the current back to the plateau. Here you'll encounter large schools of jacks and barracuda. Watch the blue for patrolling grey reef sharks, hammerheads and tuna. Along the edge of the plateau are several overhangs and small caves that shelter Napoleonfish and malabar groupers.

Location: 16km (10 miles) northeast of Wadi Gamal

Depth Range: 15-40m+ (50-130ft+)

Access: Live-aboard

Expertise Rating: Advanced

The reeftop is home to several beautiful ergs, the biggest of which, found on the west side, is covered with gorgonians. You may see schooling pelagics, turtles and whitetip reef sharks. The current can be quite strong on this side, so watch your depth and keep plenty of air in reserve for your return to the boat.

Divers fan out to look for sharks and pelagics atop the southwest plateau.

78 Sha'ab Shirinat

Between the shore and Wadi Gamal Island are three long, thin reefs that run east-west. The south side of these reefs offers sheltered anchorage from the prevailing winds, while diving takes place on the north side, which features a series of beautiful coral gardens.

A moderate current often runs from north to south, so divers usually drop in on the exposed side and drift back over the coral gardens and between the reefs. Several ergs covered in soft corals dot the north slope, which drops gradually from 10 to 30m. You'll see schools of bannerfish, groupers and angelfish. Also look for moray eels and pairs of stellate rabbitfish, as well as dragonets, goatfish and bluespotted

Location: Inshore of Wadi Gamal Island

Depth Range: 10-30m (33-100ft)

Access: Live-aboard

Expertise Rating: Intermediate

stingrays in the sand. Turtles are occasional visitors. In shallower water sohal surgeonfish, parrotfish and unicornfish swoop across the reef at great speed and will entertain you during your safety stop.

In calm weather, nearby **Habili Wadi Gamal** makes an excellent alternative dive.

The seascape at Sha'ab Shirinat boasts a spectacular range of shapes and colors.

Fury Shoal to St. John's Reef

Fury Shoal comprises a large system of reefs growing atop a shallow shelf that stretches 13km (8 miles) offshore to the north of Ras Banas. There are a number of great sites, some fairly exposed and others in calm, sheltered lagoons. Red Sea Diving Safari operates a seaside camp at Marsa Wadi Lahami to take advantage of the pristine diving along the coast and on the Fury Shoal reefs. Its fast boats can reach most of the best sites, weather permitting.

Just 16km (10 miles) north of the Sudanese border, St. John's Reef is the southernmost Egyptian reef and one of the best. There are many different dive sites, and many more to be discovered. Corals are in mint condition and the fish life thriving, including unusual species such as bumphead parrotfish. St. John's also features several spectacular ergs and habilis, with walls that vanish into deep water—natural magnets for fish shoals and pelagic species. Access is currently by liveaboard only.

GAVIN ANDERSON
Life thrives along St. John's steep walls.

Fury Shoal to St. John's Reef Dive Sites

	Good Snorkeling	Novice	Intermediate	Advanced
79 Habili Hamada	●	●		
80 *Hamada*	●	●		
81 Sha'ab Abu Galawa	●		●	
82 Sha'ab Claude (El Malahi)	●		●	
83 Sha'ab Mansour			●	
84 Sataya (Dolphin Reef)	●		●	
85 Erg Abu Diab & Eroug Abu Diab			●	
86 Petrol Tanker			●	
87 Mikauwa Island			●	
88 White Rock	●		●	
89 St. John's Reef	●		●	

79 Habili Hamada

Seven fantastic ergs reach almost to the surface from a sandy bottom between 15 and 20m. The ergs are covered with healthy hard and soft corals, as well as fire corals, and team with a wide variety of fish life. Each erg is unique, and it's usually possible to see the neighboring ergs, so navigation is fairly simple.

When crossing the sand between the ergs, look for eagle rays, shoals of fusiliers and occasionally double-lined mackerel, which patrol the ergs in search of fry amid the plankton. Porcupinefish are common visitors, as are parrotfish and large groupers, which wait patiently at cleaning stations. Shoaling anthias are abundant.

Currents are usually mild here, making this a relaxing spot for that third, late-afternoon dive.

Location: 10km (6 miles) northwest of Sha'ab Abu Galawa

Depth Range: 15-20m (50-65ft)

Access: Boat or live-aboard

Expertise Rating: Novice

GAVIN ANDERSON

Look for porcupinefish amid the hard corals.

80 *Hamada*

Atop one of the inshore reefs just east of Habili Hamada is the wreck of this 65m cargo ship. The ship was on its way from Jeddah to Suez with a cargo of polyethylene granules (a packaging and insulation product subject to wild price swings), when she sank under suspicious circumstances on June 29, 1993. The official record of the ship's loss

Location: Just north of Marsa Wadi Lahami

Depth Range: 6-14m (20-46ft)

Access: Boat or live-aboard

Expertise Rating: Novice

GAVIN ANDERSON

The *Hamada* lies just 14m (46ft) deep—perfect for novice divers and snorkelers.

Exploring Shipwrecks

Penetration by divers can accelerate a wreck's deterioration. Even minor and inadvertent contact can cause structural damage. Divers' bubbles can cause active corrosion of fragile iron bulkheads and other structures, especially where marine growth and protective sediments are damaged or disturbed.

Also remember that wreck penetration is a skilled specialty that should only be attempted by properly trained divers. Wrecks are often unstable, and they can be silty, deep and disorienting. Have an experienced guide show you wreck artifacts and the amazing coral communities that grow on them.

GAVIN ANDERSON

states that when the ship caught fire, the crew abandoned her, after which the *Hamada* hit the reef and sank. Her crew escaped in a lifeboat with enough time to take personal items and tools with them.

The wreck lies on her starboard side at the base of a shallow reef in just 14m. Bathed in sunlight, it's a very photogenic wreck. You can either circle the ship or enter the cargo holds to see the pallets of polyethylene granules suspended on the walls. You can also explore the bridge, though most of the interesting parts have been removed. A forklift lies on the sand toward the bow. Coral growth is limited to the ship's hull, but many fish are flocking to the wreck.

81 Sha'ab Abu Galawa

Abu Galawa is a large, horseshoe-shaped reef offering sheltered anchorage and excellent shallow diving. The main attraction for divers is the wreck of a tugboat, the *Tienstin*, which sank here in the 1950s. She rests against a small section of reef just south of the main reef itself. Her stern lies at 18m, while her bow almost breaks the surface and hides

Location: Fury Shoal, just east of Marsa Wadi Lahami

Depth Range: 12-20m (39-65ft)

Access: Boat or live-aboard

Expertise Rating: Intermediate

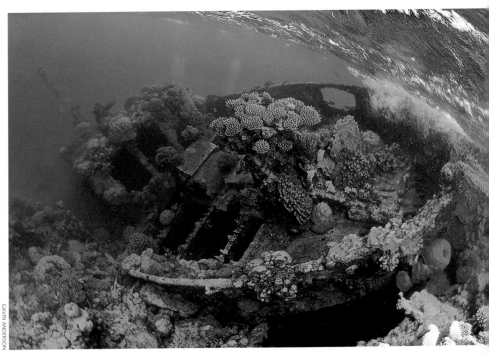

GAVIN ANDERSON

Divers can explore the tugboat *Tienstin* and several caves that dot the reef.

the entrance to a shallow cave. More-experienced divers can penetrate the forward cabin and deep inside the engine room, though it's safer to simply enjoy the wreck's external beauty.

The wreck has become a coral-festooned extension of the reef. Many fish make their home inside the wreck, while others spend time weaving throughout the corals in search of a meal. Keep an eye out for parrotfish, groupers, bannerfish and emperor and regal angelfish.

After exploring the wreck, search through several caves, both astern of the wreck and on the opposite side of the small reef. Air permitting, you could check out the main reef, a short distance north.

82 Sha'ab Claude (El Malahi)

Sha'ab Claude's alternate name, El Malahi, is Arabic for "The Playground," which aptly describes this reef riddled with whimsical caves and passages. Boats usually anchor amid a group of small coral heads on the south end of the reef.

Divers descend to 20m and follow a sandy bottom alongside the reef. Heading west past a small erg, you'll reach a coral garden boasting table corals and purple *Porites*. You'll soon see another reef dead ahead, but keep to your right and swim between the two reefs through a passage carved with overhangs and canyons. Look to

Location: Fury Shoal, 5km (3.1 miles) east of Sha'ab Abu Galawa

Depth Range: 15-22m (50-72ft)

Access: Boat or live-aboard

Expertise Rating: Intermediate

your right to spot a field of anemones and clownfish. Also watch for schools of bannerfish and goatfish, whitetip reef sharks and Napoleonfish, as well as bluespotted stingrays foraging in the sand.

As you return to the boat, look for one of two entrances to the cave system. A maze of shallow tunnels cuts into the reef, varying in depth between 5 and 10m. Open to the surface in many places, they are safe to explore.

Nearby is another excellent site named **Sha'ab Shams**, where coral ergs covered in colorful soft corals attract many reef fish and occasionally hammerhead sharks.

GAVIN ANDERSON

Goatfish use chopstick-like barbels to drive prey from the reef.

83 Sha'ab Mansour

This long, irregularly shaped reef lies on the eastern outer edge of Fury Shoal. The reef is flanked by sheer walls that plunge to great depths. The walls here are not as colorful as those at Elphinstone, and most of the diving takes place on the two plateaus at either end of the reef. Strong currents can make this an advanced dive.

Location: Fury Shoal, 6km (3.7 miles) northeast of Sha'ab Claude

Depth Range: 17-40m+ (56-130ft+)

Access: Boat or live-aboard

Expertise Rating: Intermediate

Dives typically take place on the less-exposed south plateau, which slopes gradually from 17 to 40m, where it tumbles into very deep water. Shoals of snappers, barracuda, surgeonfish and goatfish inhabit the plateau, while large Napoleonfish, trevallies and the odd grey reef shark cruise the lip of the drop-off.

Three coral towers reach from atop the plateau to within 8 or 9m of the surface. Decorated in lush soft corals and large sea fans, they are home to glassfish and groupers, which hide within the many cracks and crevices. Spend your safety stop hovering atop these miniature mountains, watching tiny blennies pop their heads in and out of holes in the coral.

A blenny's funny face is no bigger than a fingernail.

84 Sataya (Dolphin Reef)

At the southeast tip of Fury Shoal, Sataya offers ample sheltered anchorage and several large turquoise lagoons, which dolphins often frequent. Diving usually takes place on the east and south sides of the reef, along the sheer drop-off and atop a shallow plateau respectively. Just north of the main reef are several habilis, which offer even better diving in fair weather.

Location: Fury Shoal, 11km (6.8 miles) south of Sha'ab Mansour

Depth Range: 4-40m+ (13-130ft+)

Access: Boat or live-aboard

Expertise Rating: Intermediate

The east wall is wreathed in hard and soft corals, along with sea whips and gorgonians. Huge barracuda, tuna and trevallies cruise the reeftop, diving into shoals of anchovies and fusiliers, only to fall prey to the occasional whitetip and grey reef shark. The stronger the current, the more fish action you'll encounter.

In bad weather, diving shifts to the sheltered, shallow south plateau, where small coral towers reach almost to the surface. The corals are rather battered-looking close to the drop-off, but in the shallower sections they are quite healthy and boast lush soft-coral growth. Sting-rays hover along the sandy bottom, while schools of bannerfish, goatfish and yellow snappers swim amid the coral jungle.

Night diving is excellent at Sataya. Dives are usually made along the shallow plateau, where you may find Spanish dancers, sleeping parrotfish, crabs and countless shrimp.

How About a Nightcap?

You may have to wrestle into a cold, damp wetsuit, but a night dive in the Red Sea is a special experience you won't want to miss. At night the sea is a surreal place, where plankton drifts and tiny fry dance in front of your lights, fish sleep in strange cocoons and giant Spanish dancer nudibranchs perform amazing ballets.

Other nocturnal creatures to watch for include tiny sea snails and spider crabs, slipper lobsters and squid, the masters of camouflage and color changes. You may also find sleeping parrotfish and wrasses, numerous prickly sea urchins and huge basket stars that quickly curl into a ball if you shine your light on them.

Night diving does pose certain risks, however, especially at the end of a long day of repetitive diving. Take special precautions such as staying shallow, using a light with fresh batteries and taking at least one backup light per buddy pair. It is better to dive in a buddy pair at night rather than a group, and it's important to take things slowly, watch one's buoyancy control and not stir up the bottom.

GAVIN ANDERSON

85 Erg Abu Diab & Eroug Abu Diab

Erg Abu Diab (nicknamed "Erg Spice" after the Spice Girls) consists of an amazing pinnacle that rises from extremely deep water almost to the surface.

Its sheer walls are blessed with a rich variety of hard and soft corals, sea fans and sponges and attract a wide variety of fish, from large shoals of fusiliers to surgeonfish, parrotfish and unicornfish. Schools of hammerheads gather here in the summer, while whitetip and grey reef sharks are common year-round.

Location: 5km (3 miles) south of Sataya

Depth Range: 1-40m+ (3.3-130ft+)

Access: Boat or live-aboard

Expertise Rating: Intermediate

A morning dive at Erg Abu Diab is often followed by an afternoon dive at nearby Eroug Abu Diab. Here the main reef drops sharply to about 14m, where a sandy plateau slopes to a drop-off at 25m. Look for a number of huge towers amid an unusual coral garden and end your dive exploring several shallow caves close to the mooring.

86 Petrol Tanker

While still relatively unknown and rarely dived, this wreck will surely become popular in future. At present only the stern and part of the midsection have been found. Lying partly on her starboard side between 15 and 30m, the wreck is in good condition and is a fantastic sight when sunlight sweeps her decks.

Advanced coral growth suggests the ship has been underwater a long time. It's thought the tanker dates from the early 1940s and was likely torpedoed about the same time. It's possible that her bow sank quickly, perhaps several hundred meters from where the remainder of the wreck now rests.

Fish life is superb and includes large groupers and big shoals of parrotfish that graze on algae-covered sections of the ship's deck. A lone pristine table coral stands strangely sus-

Location: 16km (10 miles) north of Ras Banas

Depth Range: 15-30m (50-100ft)

Access: Boat or live-aboard

Expertise Rating: Intermediate

pended from the midsection where the ship split in two.

GAVIN ANDERSON

This table coral marks the midsection of the WWII-era petrol tanker.

87 Mikauwa Island

Dive boats enjoy the luxury of sheltered moorings at Mikauwa Island, where a coral garden comprising interesting table corals and spectacular soft corals leads to a drop-off at 20m. Look among the coral heads for bannerfish, angelfish, rainbow wrasses and moray eels.

Location: Just south of Ras Banas

Depth Range: 5-40m+ (16-130ft+)

Access: Boat or live-aboard

Expertise Rating: Intermediate

Below one of the moorings, between 20 and 40m, lies the intact wreck of an old fishing trawler—its history as yet undiscovered. A pail, spade, rope and other relics lie scattered atop the reef, suggesting the ship must have run aground before slipping into deeper water.

Night dives are popular here and offer chances to spot Spanish dancers and lots of sleeping parrotfish.

88 White Rock

Amid several scattered reefs in Foul Bay, White Rock gets its name from a huge guano-stained boulder that's visible from a distance.

Location: 24km (15 miles) south of Ras Banas

Depth Range: 5-40m+ (16-130ft+)

Access: Boat or live-aboard

Expertise Rating: Intermediate

Here a circular fringing reef encloses a turquoise lagoon. The reef drops to 15m, where a gradually sloping plateau meets a wall that drops below 40m. Several beautiful coral towers reach toward the surface, harboring butterflyfish, bannerfish and angelfish, while glassfish and squirrelfish shelter in nearby shallow caves. Grey reef sharks are occasional visitors, as are Napoleonfish and large groupers.

A few kilometers south of White Rock, **Gota White Rock** is even more dramatic, with steep walls that plunge well below the sport-diving limit. A small plateau on the southwest end offers a vantage point from which to spot tuna, mackerel and the occasional grey and whitetip reef sharks cruising by in the blue water.

89 St. John's Reef

St. John's is some 21km long by 13km wide. As this massive reef system is so remote, many dive sites were only recently explored. The reefs rise up from an enormous undersea plateau, offering virtually no protection to dive boats, but boasting exceptional diving.

In general, you'll see fish in greater numbers here than you would farther north. Divers regularly spot grey and whitetip reef sharks patrolling the reef, while hammerheads, threshers and even oceanic whitetips pay an occasional visit. You may even spot bumphead parrotfish, a species normally found farther south in Sudan.

Location: 16km (10 miles) north of the Sudanese border

Depth Range: Surface-40m+ (130ft+)

Access: Live-aboard

Expertise Rating: Intermediate

From the surface **Four-Meter Reef** (also known as **Habili Ga'afar**) looks like you could swim around it in five minutes. But once below you'll find a vast undersea island covered with beautiful purple and orange soft corals, black coral bushes and spectacular gorgonians. The walls plunge away sharply on all sides, attracting pelagic species, including sharks, to prey on the weak and injured.

Huge shoals of fish congregate around the pinnacle, with fusiliers, surgeonfish and unicornfish swarming together for feeding frenzies. In the shallows you'll find groupers, regal angelfish, shoals of bannerfish and millions of orange anthias wending their way through the dense coral growth.

Sha'ab Martin is a circular reef named for *Ghazala Voyager* skipper Martin de Banks, a well-respected European live-aboard captain who operated in the Red Sea. Its walls are adorned with black coral forests and stunning sea fans, thick with shoals of fusiliers, redtooth triggerfish, bannerfish and butterflyfish. Turtles gorge themselves on sponges and corals, while Napoleonfish cruise the reeftop. Be aware that some boats refer to Sha'ab Martin as **Sha'ab Ayman**, after a different dive boat captain.

Sha'ab Farag is another large circular reef. A huge overhang dominates a plateau on its south end, while its east wall features

a network of caves joined by a short tunnel. Look nearby for a huge field of anemones and resident clownfish.

Sha'ab Mharus is a fairly large reef riddled with caves that also boasts sheer walls adorned in beautiful sea whips and soft corals.

GAVIN ANDERSON

Delicate gorgonian sea fans lace St. John's remote walls.

Offshore Marine Park Islands

The National Marine Park islands of The Brothers, Daedalus, Zabargad and Rocky are high on divers' lists. Those who haven't been want to go, and those who have are eager to return. These islands offer some of the best diving in the world, with amazing walls festooned in soft corals and teeming with fish. The chances of seeing dolphins, sharks and unusual oceangoing fish such as sunfish are good, especially at certain times of the year.

The best shark encounters typically happen before the water has fully warmed up, in late spring, early summer and autumn—but there aren't any hard and fast rules. The sharks do disappear for periods. When conditions are right at The Brothers, Daedalus and Rocky, it's possible to see threshers, hammerheads, greys, reef whitetips, oceanic whitetips and silvertips all on one dive, though you would be a very lucky and happy diver if you did.

GAVIN ANDERSON

A crew of four still mans the 19th century lighthouse at Daedalus Reef, 96km (60 miles) offshore.

Offshore Marine Park Islands Dive Sites	Good Snorkeling	Novice	Intermediate	Advanced
90 The Brothers	●			●
91 Daedalus Reef	●			●
92 Zabargad	●			●
93 Rocky Island				●

Although sharks are much on every diver's mind, there are some interesting wrecks on Big Brother and around Zabargad. Some of the wrecks off Zabargad have just been discovered.

The islands have been given National Marine Park status. Special permission and numerous licenses are required to visit them, and the number and type of boats permitted to do so are strictly controlled. Live-aboards usually leave from Hurghada. Trips to the islands typically last two weeks, though a few companies offer 10-day trips.

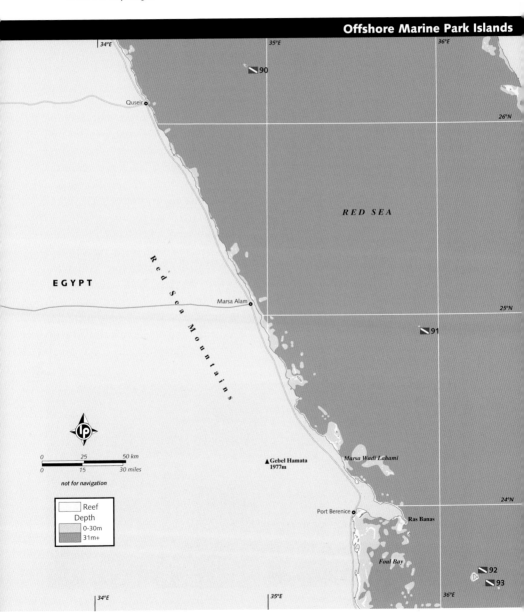

Offshore Marine Park Islands

90 The Brothers

The Brothers are two tiny islands smack in the middle of nowhere. **Big Brother** is just 400m long but dwarfs its smaller neighbor, 1km to the southeast. A lighthouse built by the British in 1880 stands 31m high on the larger of the two islands, where most boats moor overnight. The island is otherwise featureless and rather barren.

Topside views may seem a little bleak, but underwater the scenery is awesome. A fringing reef plunges away on all sides, its sheer walls covered with fantastic soft and hard corals and beautiful sea fans. Shoaling anthias dominate the scene, while jacks and tuna cruise in from the blue to prey on them and the many other tiny reef fish. Sharks such as hammerheads and greys often patrol the north end of the island and along the west wall.

The remains of an old English freighter, the *Numidia*, which sank in July 1901 after hitting the reef, rest on the north tip between 8 and 80m. Apart from the topsides and midsection, the wreck is well preserved and fairly intact. Encrusted in

Location: 67km (42 miles) east of Quseir

Depth Range: Surface-40m+ (130ft+)

Access: Live-aboard

Expertise Rating: Advanced

spectacular soft corals and teeming with fish, she is a very colorful and exciting wreck to dive on. A pair of old locomotive wheels lies at the top of the wreck, suggesting her initial cargo and lending her the nickname "The Locomotive Wreck."

Most divers explore halfway down the wreck to about 40m, where views toward the surface are breathtaking. With plenty of air, it's possible to return to your boat with the current along the west wall. On the way back you'll find interesting overhangs and small caves filled with thousands of glassfish.

Coral-encased locomotive wheels cap the remains of the *Numidia*.

GAVIN ANDERSON

You'll also come across the remains of another wreck, the *Aida II*, an Egyptian troop transport that sank in 1957 while trying to secure its mooring. She has since broken into two. Part of the ship, including the engine block, lies scattered in shallow water at the top of the reef, while the largely intact main section is between 30 and 60m. Like the *Numidia*, the *Aida* is adorned with soft corals and is also home to a large shoal of glassfish. Due to its depth, this wreck really needs to be explored on a separate dive.

Little Brother is a magical island, rated by many as the best dive site in the Red Sea. The circular reef looks tiny from the surface, but plateaus on its north and south ends extend far underwater. The north plateau shelves sharply from just a few meters to 30 and then 45m, while the south plateau slopes to 45m.

The island's sheer walls are festooned with gigantic soft corals, sea fans and amazing black coral bushes. Fish seem to be everywhere, from orange anthias to shoals of snappers, tuna, barracuda, triggerfish and Napoleonfish.

But what divers are most interested in seeing are the sharks. There are few places in the world where you can swim with so many different species. Greys, whitetips, silvertips, hammerheads and threshers are all present when conditions are right. One can become quite overwhelmed by the shark action and forget to enjoy the island's amazing underwater scenery and other fish life.

The sharks tend to cruise the north plateau, where the current can get quite strong. Divers drop in from Zodiacs to watch the action from the northeast edge of the plateau before drifting back to the boat.

Whale sharks, manta rays and occasionally oceangoing fish pass by Little Brother, and oceanic whitetips have been known to swim right up to the stern of dive boats.

GAVIN ANDERSON

Though sharks steal the show, Little Brother boasts a lush reef.

91 Daedalus Reef (Abu el-Kizan)

Small, isolated Daedalus Reef, also known as Abu el-Kizan, lies right in the middle of the Red Sea, nearly halfway to Saudi Arabia. As it is so isolated, dive boats avoid the island in all but the best weather conditions.

Location: 96km (60 miles) off Marsa Alam

Depth Range: Surface-40m+ (130ft+)

Access: Live-aboard

Expertise Rating: Advanced

The reef is almost round, reaching about 500m at its widest point. A 19th century lighthouse built by the British stands high in the middle of the reef on a small patch of sand and is the only reference point for miles around. It's still run by a crew of four, who receive supplies once a month. Boats moor off the southern side of the reef, which offers the best shelter from the north winds.

As you'd expect on a reef in the middle of nowhere, fish life is quite good, with shoals of fusiliers, snappers, spotted unicornfish and surgeonfish. You may also spot the occasional turtle.

Like all the offshore National Marine Park islands, Daedalus has spectacular sheer walls, carpeted with soft and hard corals as well as sea fans. The walls drop sharply on all sides except to the south, where there is a plateau between 30 and 40m, home to resident greys and threshers. The east wall is carved with overhangs and caves, where large groupers often rest. The west wall features soft- and hard-coral formations, as well as a large field of beautiful anemones and clownfish, which easily rank with those at Ras Mohammed's Anemone City.

The most popular spot to dive, however, is along the north wall, where strong currents attract schooling barracuda, jacks, tuna, rainbow runners and hammerheads. The remains of at least one shipwreck lie here.

GAVIN ANDERSON

A soft-coral tree unfurls from the wall to feed.

92 | Zabargad

The largest island for miles around, Zabargad offers good shelter for boats. In years past the pharaohs, Romans and, more recently, modern Egyptians mined a green mineral called olivine here. Today Zabargad is a tranquil island with a beautiful turquoise lagoon. The triangular island covers 5 sq km, with large pointed hills dominating its interior. Its beaches attract nesting turtles, which divers often encounter, especially in August.

Diving takes place on the sheltered south side, where fantastic coral pillars join together to form a mini-wall riddled with winding passages. A sandy slope runs gradually down to 20m before plunging over a sheer wall. The slope is dotted with beautiful coral towers, each with its own character.

Angelfish, butterflyfish, groupers and moray eels are particularly prevalent, as are bluespotted stingrays and scorpionfish, which hide in the sand. Jacks and the odd tuna cruise along the top of the wall, while leopard and nurse sharks sometimes rest on the sandy plateau.

Several shipwrecks lie offshore, including the **Neptune**, a German dive boat that had starter problems and was blown onto the reef in bad weather on April 29, 1981. Its remains lie scattered between 15 and 30m along a steep sloping reef. Nearby is the largely intact wreckage of a 70m freighter, the history of which remains unknown.

Location: 46km (29 miles) south of Ras Banas

Depth Range: 10-40m+ (33-130ft+)

Access: Live-aboard

Expertise Rating: Advanced

MARK WEBSTER

Groupers fare well along the offshore islands' coral-rich reef slopes.

93 Rocky Island

Exposed Rocky Island, with its noisy seabirds and breaking waves, lies just north of the Sudanese border and is one of Egypt's most remote dive sites. With strong currents, big swells and active sharks, diving at Rocky is an extremely exciting experience.

The reef is somewhat kidney-shaped, capped by a beautiful shallow reeftop that shelters many strange and familiar reef fish. It drops sharply from just a few meters below the surface to incredible depths. Its walls are covered in soft corals, sponges and giant sea fans, interrupted on the northeast and southeast corners by a narrow shelf at 25m—the perfect platform from which to watch all the surrounding action. Tall, dangling sea whips sprout from deeper water, and several fantastic overhangs and caves complete the weird and wonderful scene.

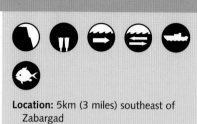

Location: 5km (3 miles) southeast of Zabargad

Depth Range: Surface-40m+ (130ft+)

Access: Live-aboard

Expertise Rating: Advanced

The southeast corner is considered the best place to find sharks and pelagics. Divers have encountered patrolling greys, massive hammerheads and silvertips, as well as mantas, oceanic whitetips, whale sharks and even the occasional sailfish.

When dive conditions are perfect, it's possible to see just about anything both underwater and on the surface. Divers often jump right back into the water after a dive to snorkel with dolphins.

GAVIN ANDERSON

Open-water currents promote coral growth on a grand scale.

Southern Red Sea Dive Sites

No Red Sea dive guide would be complete without some mention of the southern sites, which in fact constitute more than half of the region's diving potential. Although diving in Sudan, Eritrea, Yemen and Djibouti is difficult, windows of opportunity occur from time to time that allow divers to sample some of the region's rare delights. Indeed, it is the difficulties in accessing the region that ensure the reefs remain unspoiled by human traffic.

The late 1980s and early '90s saw one large window of opportunity, and boats like the *Lady Jenny V* and *Poseidon's Quest* spent several years cruising the coast, relatively unhindered. During the summer months they would return to Egypt to shelter from the heat. Ironically, it was Egypt's attempts to shove out foreign competition—and not unrest in the south—that put an end to those dive trips.

Since then Eritrea and Yemen have disputed ownership of the Hanish and Zubayr groups, and Eritrea has waged an on-off border war with Ethiopia. For a while Sudan was out-of-bounds due to U.S. missile attacks in the wake of the Kenyan embassy bombing. But positive signs are starting to emerge. Yemen is certainly keen to boost tourism, while Sudan is also making encouraging noises. Both countries are best approached through Italian operators, who have always been dominant in the region as a result of old colonial ties.

Commercial operations or not, there is always the option of touring the southern Red Sea by yacht. This is generally safe for citizens of countries that have not made themselves enemies of Islam, but it's not an especially bright idea for Americans or Israelis to spend too much time down there. Still, adventurous souls will be the ones that reap the rewards of venturing that little bit farther.

Moreover, politics shift like the winds in this part of the world, and you never know when a opportunity to visit will again present itself—after all, it was only several years ago that Eritrea was heavily promoting its interest in tourism. As soon as Sudan opens up properly, jump on the first boat to experience big-fish diving without equal. Sure, the Cocos, South Africa and the Galapagos may offer bigger fish and more of them, but those are generally rocky, inhospitable places. Here you'll see sharks in profusion parading before a backdrop of lush soft corals.

GAVIN ANDERSON

You won't pass many dive boats this far south.

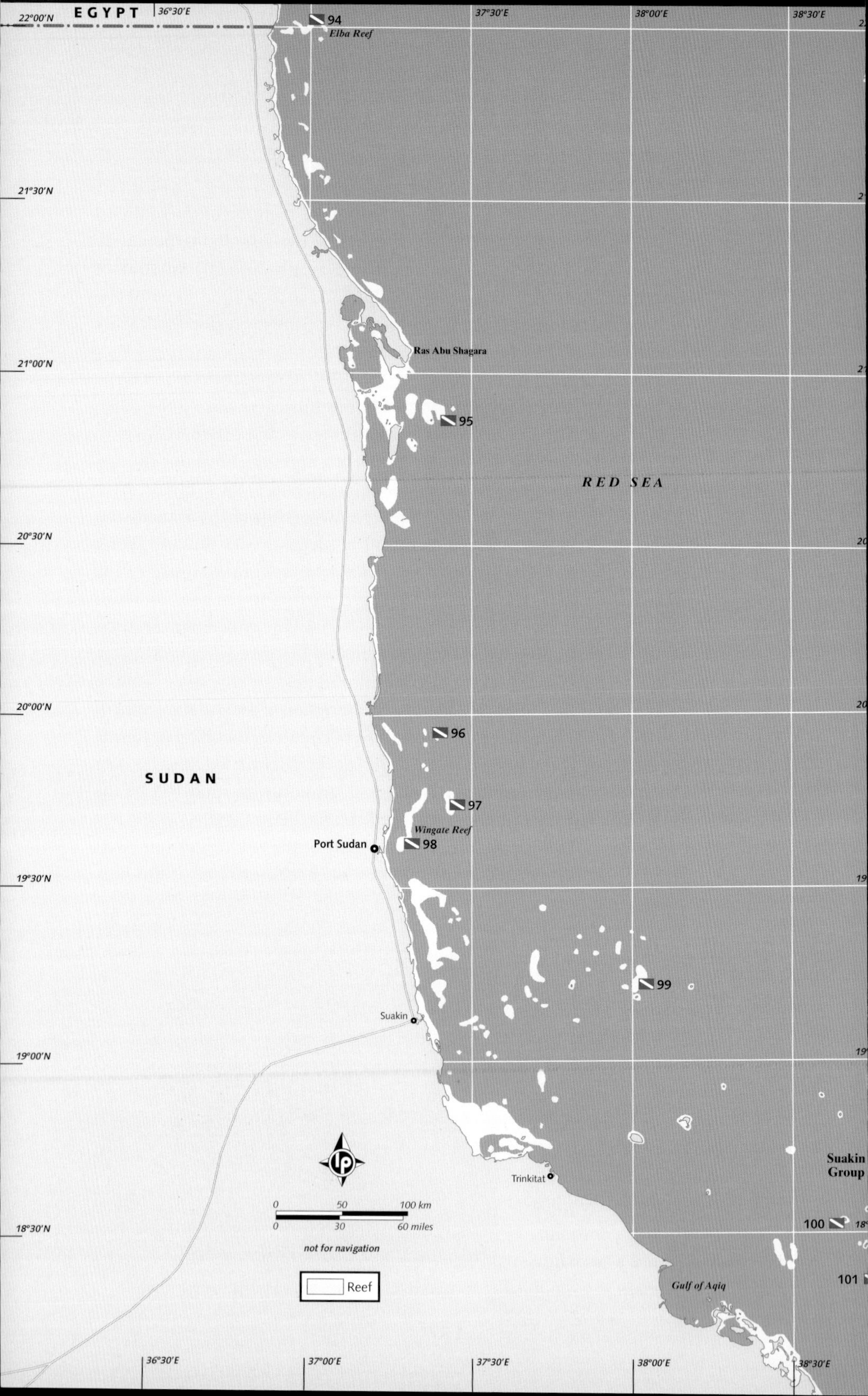

Sudan

EGYPT

36°30'E

22°00'N

94

Elba Reef

37°30'E

38°00'E

38°30'E

21°30'N

21°00'N

Ras Abu Shagara

95

RED SEA

20°30'N

SUDAN

20°00'N

96

97

Wingate Reef

Port Sudan

98

19°30'N

99

Suakin

19°00'N

Suakin
Group

Trinkitat

0   50   100 km

0   30   60 miles

100

18°30'N

not for navigation

101

Reef

Gulf of Aqiq

Sudan

Sudan Dive Sites

	Good Snorkeling	Novice	Intermediate	Advanced
94 *Lavanzo*			●	
95 Angarosh		●	●	
96 Sha'ab Rumi		●	●	
97 Sanganeb Reef		●	●	
98 *Umbria*				●
99 Protector & Preserver Reefs		●	●	
100 Dahrat Ghab		●	●	
101 Dahrat Abid		●	●	

94 *Lavanzo*

Heading down from the relatively crowded waters of Egypt into Sudan, you start to feel like early explorers must have when they headed up the Congo—this is real *Heart of Darkness* stuff. The first decent site you come to is Elba Reef and the wreck of the *Lavanzo*.

As with many of the wrecks this far south, little is known about the *Lavanzo*, but it has been suggested that a set of marble cupids recovered by an Israeli boat in the early 1990s was destined for an Italian monastery in Eritrea. Now the ship lies upside down, its back broken across the sharp drop-off of the reef.

The stern is at around 25m, with the propeller and rudder rising to about 18m, which can be used as a solid mooring point for the dive boat. There is plenty of opportunity for rummaging among wreckage that has been

Location: Northern Sudan

Depth Range: 18-40m+ (60-130ft+)

Access: Live-aboard

Expertise Rating: Intermediate

laid open by the elements, and you can still find bottles and other remnants of the cargo.

At 40m the ship is split, and from here on it slopes steeply down to about 75m and the bow. Below the sport-diving limit, this is silvertip shark territory. At one time a heavily scarred female patrolled the wreck, making no secret of her hostility to intruders. No damage was ever done, but that toothy grimace left a lasting impression among divers.

95 Angarosh

Angarosh—it's a fierce sounding name, and just as well, because it's a fierce kind of reef. The name Angarosh has become synonymous with sharks, and large numbers of them.

But not to worry: As in the rest of the Red Sea, most of the sharks here are of the passive variety—in this case hammerheads. The northeast point of Angarosh is

Location: Northern Sudan

Depth Range: 3-40m+ (10-130ft+)

Access: Live-aboard

Expertise Rating: Intermediate

GAVIN ANDERSON

Scalloped hammerhead sharks frequent the deep water off the northeast point.

where they hang out. A rocky ridge runs steeply out to sea, leveling off here and there to form wide ledges, one at 25m, another at around 40m. Below 50m it starts to rise again as a small shoal.

One Red Sea guide tells of divers being herded away from the reef and into the blue by a group of three silvertips. Silvertips are not considered to be especially dangerous. On the other hand, these three had no intention of letting

the group back to the reef and made several dummy charges each time they tried. Just as the divers' air consumption was starting to creep up, along came the cavalry—a school of 12 hammerheads, which surrounded the silvertips and chased them out to sea. The divers returned to look over their strange new-found pets and for the next 15 minutes were themselves examined from every possible angle by these curious giants.

Red Sea Shark Primer

True, the vast majority of sharks will not attack or harass humans, and even fewer will actually try to eat them. But equally, there is no denying that sharks are predators, and just a few are swimming dustbins that will have a chew on whatever comes their way. Among these are tiger sharks, silky sharks and oceanic whitetips—all of which frequent the Red Sea. To put things into context, however, these are three species found in nearly all tropical seas.

Tiger sharks are rare in the Red Sea. They are generally held to be most common in southern waters but have been sighted as far north as Dahab. Meanwhile, the despicable practice of shark-finning for Far Eastern gourmet markets keeps the numbers down in the south. Some very large specimens have been spotted in the Red Sea, but on no occasions have they caused problems.

Oceanic whitetips are, as the name suggests, oceanic sharks that spend a lot of time cruising at sea on broad, white-tipped fins that resemble aircraft wings. They prefer to remain at the surface. Living so far out in the sterile tropical oceans, they cannot afford to pass up any potential prey—including a diver. Elphinstone Reef in southern Egypt, The Brothers and Ras Mohammed experience fairly frequent encounters, which rarely result in more than a nibbled fin and the need for a change of swim trunks. The situation is not helped by people feeding these sharks from their boats.

Silky sharks are close relatives of oceanic whitetips and exhibit similar behavior and tastes. They have also jangled the nerves of a few divers floating at the surface waiting to be picked up, but these encounters are very rare. They become especially agitated at dusk and in the presence of dolphins. Sha'ab Rumi in Sudan is one prime hangout.

As a rule both silkies and oceanic whitetips nudge several times before they bite, so the floating diver gets ample warning. They often feed on sick dolphins, but since a healthy adult dolphin is capable of inflicting severe damage, they are understandably tentative. A diver is treated with similar caution. If bumped, you should get straight back aboard the boat. Failing that, you should descend and make your way to the reef below the surface, and keeping your back against the reef, climb slowly out.

You're more likely to encounter less dangerous species. Silvertips (see photo below) are territorial and can put on aggressive displays, but on the whole they are shy pussycats. Others such as hammerheads, nurse sharks, leopard sharks, grey and whitetip reef sharks, threshers, oceanic blacktips, blacktip reef sharks, sandbar sharks, dusky sharks, etc., are perfectly placid if treated with respect. Whale sharks, the world's largest fish, feed on plankton and small fish and pose no threat to divers.

LAWSON WOOD

96 | Sha'ab Rumi

Where to start, with what is undoubtedly the Red Sea's most diverse and time-consuming reef? The south plateau is as good a place as any, with shark cages left over from Cousteau's era and scores of grey reef sharks cruising eagerly up and down the plateau at the first whiff of bait. Behind them, in the blue, lurk silvertips, and often in the surface waters is the sobering proposition of silky sharks.

Farther down the plateau, a memorial plaque lends a chilling reminder of man's frailty. Schools of barracuda twist and spiral overhead, and occasionally hammerheads cruise in the currents beyond the point.

Your boat will doubtless moor in the calm of the lagoon, and it is just outside the entrance channels that Cousteau set up his underwater village Conshelf II. In

Location: Central Sudan

Depth Range: 3-40m+ (10-130ft+)

Access: Live-aboard

Expertise Rating: Intermediate

fact, it was Cousteau who blasted these channels in the first place to give his support vessels access to the lagoon. The village makes a stunning night dive, including an opportunity to surface inside the submarine garage and discuss the myriad sights that will have caught your attention. Bumphead parrotfish often roost here overnight. As a rule, sharks on the south plateau don't head up this far.

GAVIN PARSONS

In 1963 Jacques Cousteau established his Conshelf II underwater village on this reef.

97 Sanganeb Reef

Sanganeb is a long ellipse of reef with a shallow lagoon at its center and a lighthouse on its southern tip. It offers two main dive sites: a long ridge at the north end and a stunning plateau to the southwest. In the lagoon lies the wreck of the *White Elephant*—a dive boat from the early days with some colorful stories behind it.

The north ridge is much like that on the northeast point of Angarosh, tum-

Location: Central Sudan

Depth Range: 3-40m+ (10-130ft+)

Access: Live-aboard

Expertise Rating: Intermediate

A view across the lagoon from the lighthouse on Sanganeb's southern tip.

GAVIN PARSONS

bling down to a ledge and then falling again to something of a seamount at 40m and a final ledge at 55m. As at Angarosh, the morning often brings hammerheads in the blue, anywhere between 25 and 55m. Strong currents often sweep through in the afternoon.

The south plateau is a mixture of sand and soft-coral-covered pinnacles at about 25m, patrolled by grey reef sharks. Between 30 and 35m the plateau begins to slope steeply, before dropping away at 55m. Marbled groupers, jacks, barracuda and hammerheads dominate this zone.

98 *Umbria*

As Italy was about to go to war in 1940, the freighter *Umbria* was loaded with bombs, detonators and cars, bound for the busy Eritrean port of Massawa, then

Location: Central Sudan

Depth Range: 18-40m (60-130ft)

Access: Live-aboard

Expertise Rating: Advanced

GAVIN PARSONS

Umbria's cargo included Fiat 1100 Lunga cars.

Aden and Calcutta. As it headed down the Red Sea, the ship was intercepted by the British Royal Navy and forced to drop anchor at Wingate Reef, outside Port Sudan. During its detention the message went out that Italy was at war, and within moments the master had successfully scuttled the *Umbria* to keep its stores from falling into enemy hands.

Diving the ship is a delicate issue, as it is still stacked with explosives—enough to sink the whole of Port Sudan. Nevertheless, it still receives the occasional visitor. The wreck is 155m long and lies between 18 and 40m. It is often rated the best wreck dive in the Red Sea.

99 Protector & Preserver Reefs

Protector is a huge reef with a large lagoon at its center and the rusting hulk of a cargo ship stranded on its northern flanks. It was here that the *Lady Jenny V* grounded in the late 1980s, prompting an Israeli helicopter to rush down and rescue certain guests before the Sudanese got hold of them.

At the south end is a long sandy plateau that shelves gently down to a drop-off at about 20m, and this alone can justify a couple of days of diving. Between the many coral buttresses and outcrops wind sandy gullies frequented

Location: Southern Sudan

Depth Range: 3-40m (10-130ft)

Access: Live-aboard

Expertise Rating: Intermediate

by sleeping whitetip reef sharks. Their bigger cousins the oceanic whitetips occasionally cruise by in the clear waters above. Eagle rays, bumphead parrotfish, manta rays and turtles are occasional visitors. Close to the reef is a shallow sandy bay, where triggerfish nest in the early summer months, as tightly packed as seabirds. Down the west and east sides run imposing walls, but it's on the plateau that most of the fish life thrives.

Preserver Reef, several miles to the east, features a stunning wall dive along its south end, with immaculate coral gardens in the shallow waters. Huge clams are imbedded in this reef, which is riddled with swim-throughs and gullies.

100 Dahrat Ghab

Part of the southern Suakin Group, Dahrat Ghab is another insignificant-looking sandy island, topped by a wreck. But beneath the water it is crammed with life to such an extent that it's hard to know where to look.

Off the southwest end is a plateau with a sandy crescent at its center, bounded on the outside by a crescent-shaped ridge. The best dive starts on either side of this plateau, depending on the current, and drifts across the plateau to the shelter on the other side.

The ridge is a veritable fish magnet, with schools of jacks, twisting columns of barracuda and scores of snappers congregating in the waters above. The

Location: Suakin Group in southern Sudan

Depth Range: 3-40m+ (10-130ft+)

Access: Live-aboard

Expertise Rating: Intermediate

first divers to arrive at the sandy crescent often witness it being used as something of a dormitory for whitetip reef sharks. Also watch for the usual big stuff that frequents the Suakins, including hammerheads, manta rays and silvertips.

101 Dahrat Abid

Depending on conditions and the time of year, the eight Suakins come into flower one after the other. Expect the best diving this planet has to offer—pure blue water, dizzying drop-offs, as well as whitetips, silvertips and hammerheads in about the same quantities as you find anthias elsewhere in the Red Sea.

Dahrat Abid is the southernmost of the group, topped by a sandy island and a wreck. The east end of the reef is home to a magnificent thresher shark, while the walls to the south are characterized by caves, black coral bushes and a riot of color in the shallow water. This

Location: Suakin Group in southern Sudan

Depth Range: 3-40m+ (10-130ft+)

Access: Live-aboard

Expertise Rating: Intermediate

reef is best seen on a trip heading up from the south, as it's the first of the big Red Sea drop-offs you come to. Five miles to the north, **Darraka** is similar but without the wreck.

Eritrea

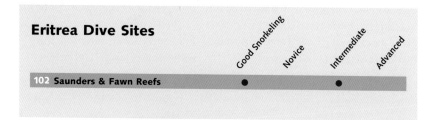

Eritrea Dive Sites

	Good Snorkeling	Novice	Intermediate	Advanced
102 Saunders & Fawn Reefs	●		●	

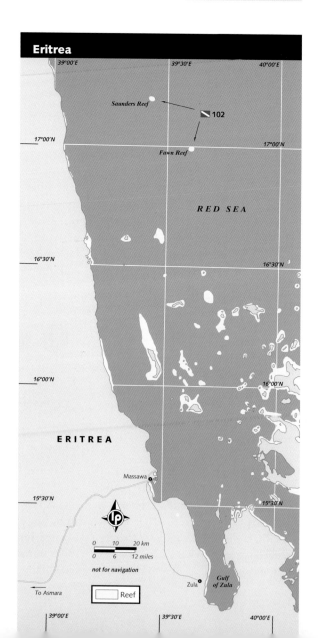

102 Saunders & Fawn Reefs

Saunders and Fawn are the last diveable reefs in Eritrean waters before you cross into Sudanese territory. They mark the divide between the shallow sandy waters of the south and the steep blue drop-offs of the north, and in character they combine certain aspects of each of the two regions.

Saunders Reef boasts a steep wall to the north that drops to 60m, and this is where divers should begin their exploration. Heading east will take you to a series of wide sandy shelves, and it's in the deep water beyond that silvertip sharks occasionally patrol. The best diving, however, is amid the shallow hard-coral gardens along the edge of the reeftop.

Location: Northern Eritrea

Depth Range: 3-40m (10-130ft)

Access: Live-aboard

Expertise Rating: Intermediate

Nearby Fawn Reef is just deep enough to moor the average dive boat. This allows for some stunning night dives, which often attract manta rays that come to feed on the plankton illuminated by divers' lights. Their white bellies are visible from the surface as they turn and somersault in the glare of the lights, occasionally silhouetted by the flash of a strobe.

GAVIN ANDERSON

When feeding, mantas extend horn-like cephalic lobes and often turn backflips to gather plankton.

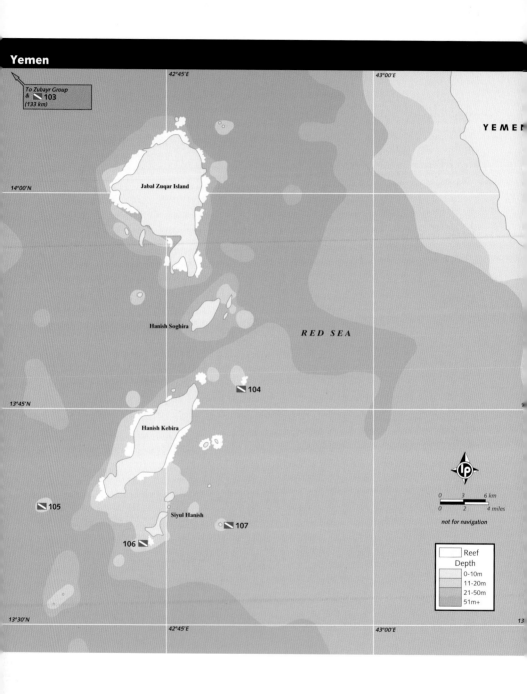

Yemen

To Zubayr Group
& 103
(133 km)

42°45'E

43°00'E

YEMEN

14°00'N

Jabal Zuqar Island

Hanish Soghira

RED SEA

13°45'N

104

Hanish Kebira

105

Siyul Hanish

107

106

13°30'N

42°45'E

43°00'E

0   3   6 km
0   2   4 miles

not for navigation

Reef
Depth
0-10m
11-20m
21-50m
51m+

Yemen

Yemen Dive Sites	Good Snorkeling	Novice	Intermediate	Advanced
103 Quoin Rock	●		●	
104 Mushajirah			●	
105 Southwest Rocks			●	
106 Ship Rock	●		●	
107 Parkin Rock & Porcelain Wreck	●		●	

103 Quoin Rock

Quoin—meaning corner in medieval English—is an apt description of this angular sandstone buttress in the Zubayr island group.

Location: Zubayr Group in northern Yemen

Depth Range: 3-40m (10-130ft)

Access: Live-aboard

Expertise Rating: Intermediate

The northeast point is the easiest place to moor and, coincidentally, marks the starting point of the best dive. Beneath the boat, a long ridge slopes gently down to a dome, before shelving away steeply to depths of 60m plus, where a sandy slope begins—home to a hefty-looking silvertip shark.

Traverse the drop-off at about 40m, before returning up the side of the ridge to circle the island at about 12m. At that depth you'll run straight into the gully that splits the rock at about 10m, providing a stunning, surge-washed swim-through. Around

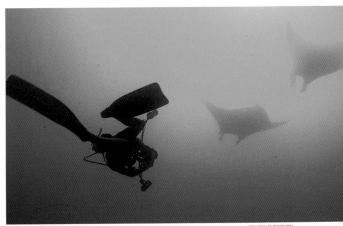

GAVIN ANDERSON

Let fast-cruising manta rays come to you—pursuit is futile.

the south end of the rock is a cluster of beautiful coral-encrusted boulders—great for photography and also the location of numerous manta sightings.

104 Mushajirah

Mushajirah is a crescent of exposed reef topped by two rocky pinnacles. It's also the resting place of an ancient steamship rumored to be a sister ship of the world-renowned *Carnatic*. The wreck lies on the exposed south slope of the reef at about 25m and is home to one of the biggest and most inquisitive giant groupers in the region, which must weigh all of 135kg.

Divers are best advised to enter the water from a Zodiac, in line with the easternmost pinnacle. The first thing you'll come across is a region of ballast and assorted junk, amid which various shabby trophies have been found. From here follow the 25m mark east until you bump into the wreck and its fat-lipped inhabitant.

After touring the wreck, return to the shallow waters, which are literally crawl-

Location: Hanish Group in central Yemen

Depth Range: 3-30m (10-100ft)

Access: Live-aboard

Expertise Rating: Intermediate

ing with lobsters, usually at around 7m. Keep an eye on the waters above for schools of mobulas (rays related to the manta) that often glide by. A shallow plateau at about 5m blocks your return to the boat, which has doubtless moored in the deep lagoon inside the crescent. Crossing the plateau will take you past several plumes of coral debris, shattered by the heavy seas and washed onto the reeftop.

105 Southwest Rocks

Southwest Rocks encapsulates all the charm of the region, while adding a depth factor missing from other sites. From the surface it looks like a small rocky strip, split down the middle by a shallow gully. Where you start your dive depends on where sea conditions allow you to tie up your boat, but all sides of the reef are excellent.

Start at the east end of the reef, following the ledges that step down the north slope. The current often rips up from the south, thundering through the shallow gully at the middle of the reef to cascade down the other side. Dolphins

Location: Hanish Group in central Yemen

Depth Range: 3-40m (10-130ft)

Access: Live-aboard

Expertise Rating: Intermediate

sometimes play in this jet of current, apparently racing up the reef and then riding down on the stream.

At the western point of the reef are a set of pinnacles and a shoulder of coral

GAVIN ANDERSON

Marine life is particularly prevalent off the western point at Southwest Rocks.

and rock that tumbles down to ledges at the 40 to 50m mark. This area is forested with sea fans, sea whips and black corals and heavily populated with shoals of jacks, oceanic triggerfish and various other species.

One Red Sea guide tells of a diver who took shelter from the current here behind a rocky outcrop. Suddenly, it went dark, and he looked up to see the belly of a small whale shark inching slowly by only a meter above. Seemingly minutes later the end of its tail merged into the shimmering water, and it disappeared. Dives here have yielded encounters with other striking critters—from aggressive baby silvertips to mind-boggling nudibranchs.

Encounters with whale sharks are rare and memorable.

106 Ship Rock

Several kilometers southwest of Siyul Hanish is a vast expanse of glassy nothingness, with no sign of a reef for miles. Only when the tide switches and currents start to rip does the sea begin to bulge at this watery outpost, and whitecaps betray the reef beneath.

And not just a reef—Ship Rock is the scene of an ancient grounding. The ship must have perched aloft for some time before breaking its back and settling to the sand on either side. The stern is the more picturesque of the two parts. Thoroughly obscured in a coat of ferny white corals and cloaked in shoals of sweetlips, it stretches down to 18m.

On the sand around the wreck, leopard blennies have made their burrows,

Location: Hanish Group in central Yemen

Depth Range: 3-25m (10-80ft)

Access: Live-aboard

Expertise Rating: Intermediate

which they share with bulldozer shrimp. Nurse and whitetip reef sharks are so commonplace as to hardly merit a second glance. Morays, snappers and huge silvery pompano are among the other residents. If you're sailing through the Hanish Group, this site should top your diving itinerary.

107 Parkin Rock & Porcelain Wreck

This remote guano-stained outcrop is typical of Yemeni diving—uninspiring at the surface, but awe-inspiring beneath. The rocky projection is just the summit of a long ridge stretching east-west, with superb shallow diving in either direction. It's on the southeast side, however, that you find the justification for coming this far. A small ship lies shattered across the reef, its engine room lying in shallow water with the boilers falling just short of the surface. The bow lies almost intact on the sand to the east.

The cargo of porcelain—saki bowls, plates and vases—lies scattered and buried in the sand for hundreds of yards around. Only after severe winter storms sweep the rock are these objects unearthed, and the first yacht to visit in the

Location: Hanish Group in central Yemen

Depth Range: 3-25m (10-82ft)

Access: Live-aboard

Expertise Rating: Intermediate

spring often leaves loaded with rather worthless treasures.

Treasure-hunting aside, there is stunning marine life here. Schools of small barracuda and jacks circle and swirl over the sandy slopes, nurse and leopard sharks tuck themselves away under brain corals, and lobsters' antennae protrude from the many crevices.

A leopard shark and hitchhiking remora rest atop the seafloor at Parkin Rock.

Djibouti

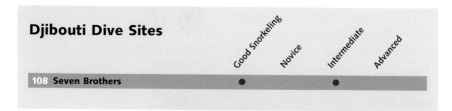

Djibouti Dive Sites

	Good Snorkeling	Novice	Intermediate	Advanced
108 Seven Brothers	●		●	

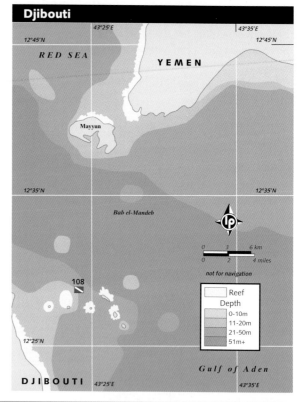

Djibouti

RED SEA

YEMEN

Mayyun

Bab el-Mandeb

108

Reef
Depth
0-10m
11-20m
21-50m
51m+

0   3   6 km
0   2   4 miles

not for navigation

Gulf of Aden

DJIBOUTI

108 Seven Brothers

This region is one of the most complex and fascinating on the face of the planet.

Trapped in the bottleneck between the Red Sea and the Gulf of Aden, the Seven Brothers bear the brunt of the raging currents that sweep through twice a day. Cold greenish water is whipped up over the rocky plateaus to nourish colorful soft corals and other creatures that feed

Location: Bab el-Mandeb Strait, off Djibouti

Depth Range: 3-40m (10-130ft)

Access: Live-aboard

Expertise Rating: Intermediate

on the plankton—including occasional whale sharks.

The seven reefs vary immensely, from **Rhounda Dhabali**, which is largely dead, to **Rhounda Khomaytou**, which is literally seething with life. There are shallow gardens such as the **Jardins Japonais** on **Kadda Dhabali**, frequented by nurse sharks, Spanish dancers and at night dozens of lobsters. There are also deep drop-offs such as the east ridge of Rhounda Khomaytou, which boasts giant groupers and oversized nudibranchs not seen anywhere else in the Red Sea. Indian Ocean species also hold their own here, with honeycomb morays, oceanic triggerfish and giant sweetlips in abundance.

GAVIN ANDERSON

Divers should use caution when approaching honeycomb morays, as adult eels may strike defensively.

MARK WEBSTER

Marine Life

Marine life in the Red Sea is renowned for its endless variety. Hard corals, soft corals, tropicals and pelagics—this natural aquarium has them all in countless numbers. Though each reef boasts prolific marine life, the species obviously vary according to location. For instance, pelagics, especially sharks, are more regularly seen in the southern Red Sea.

Though it would be impractical to list all the species you are likely to see while diving in the Red Sea, this section will identify some of the more common vertebrates and invertebrates. The next section describes potentially harmful or dangerous marine life you might encounter.

Keep in mind that common names are used freely by most divers and are often inconsistent. The two-part scientific name is much more accurate. This system is known as binomial nomenclature—the method of using two words (shown in italics) to identify an organism. The first italic word is the genus, into which members of similar species are grouped. The second word, the species, is the finest detail name and refers to organisms that are sexually compatible and can produce fertile offspring. Where the species is unknown or not yet named, the genus name is followed by *sp.*

Common Vertebrates

variegated lizardfish
Synodus variegatus

sabre squirrelfish
Sargocentron spiniferum

cornetfish
Fistularia commersonii

crocodilefish (carpet flathead)
Papilloculiceps longiceps

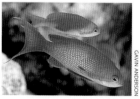

jewel fairy basslet (goldie)
Pseudanthias squamipinnis

coral grouper
Cephalopholis miniata

176

Red Sea coralgrouper
Plectropomus pessuliferus marisrubri

sixstripe soapfish
Grammistes sexlineatus

freckled hawkfish
Paracirrhites forsteri

longnose hawkfish
Oxycirrhites typus

large-toothed cardinalfish
Cheilodipterus macrodon

bigeye
Priacanthus hamrur

bigeye trevally
Caranx sexfasciatus

black-and-white snapper
Macolor niger

onespot snapper
Lutjanus monostigma

yellowfin goatfish
Mulloidichthys vanicolensis

glassfish (yellow sweepers)
Parapriacanthus ransonneti

batfish
Platax orbicularis

masked (golden) butterflyfish
Chaetodon semilarvatus

Red Sea bannerfish
Heniochus intermedius

emperor angelfish
Pomancanthus imperator

map (yellowbar) angelfish
Pomancanthus maculosus

regal angelfish
Pygoplites diacanthus

two-banded anemonefish
Amphiprion bicinctus

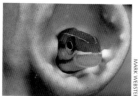

lemon damselfish
Pomacentrus sulfureus

Indo-Pacific sergeant
Abudefduf vaigensis

bicolor parrotfish
Cetoscarus bicolor

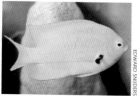

scale-eating fangblenny
Plagiotremus tapeinosoma

lemon coral goby
Gobiodon citrinus

yellow boxfish
Ostracion cubicus

star puffer
Arothron stellatus

scribbled filefish
Aluterus scriptus

blacktongue unicornfish
Naso hexacanthus

dogtooth tuna
Gymnosarda unicolor

Napoleonfish (humphead wrasse)
Cheilinus undulatus

hawksbill sea turtle
Eretmochelys imbricata

Common Invertebrates

stony coral
Acropora sp.

table coral
Acropora hyacinthus

yellow waver coral
(cabbage coral)
Turbinaria mesenterina

leather coral
Sarcophyton ehrenbergi

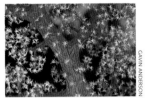

soft coral
Dendronephthya sp.

bubble anemone
Entacmaea quadricolor

pearl sea star
Fromia monilus

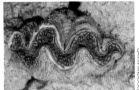

giant clam
Tridacna maxima

pyjama nudibranch
Chromodoris quadricolor

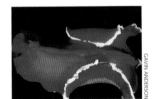

Spanish dancer
Hexabranchus sanguineus

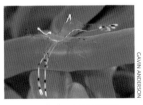

anemone partner shrimp
Periclimenes longicarpus

Durban dancing shrimp
Rhynchocinetes durbanensis

variable coral crab
Carpilius convexus

common reef octopus
Octopus cyaneus

cuttlefish
Sepia sp.

Hazardous Marine Life

Marine animals almost never attack divers, but many have defensive and offensive weaponry that can be triggered if they feel threatened or annoyed. The ability to recognize hazardous creatures is a valuable asset in avoiding injury. Following are some of the potentially hazardous creatures most commonly found in the Red Sea.

Shark

Sharks come in many shapes and sizes. They are most recognizable by their triangular dorsal fin. Though many species are shy, there are occasional attacks. About 25 species worldwide are considered dangerous to humans. Those occurring in the Red Sea include the tiger, oceanic whitetip, silky and silvertip sharks. Sharks will generally not attack unless provoked, so don't taunt, tease or feed them.

GAVIN ANDERSON

Avoid spearfishing, carrying fish baits or mimicking a wounded fish and your likelihood of being attacked will greatly diminish. Face and quietly watch any shark that is acting aggressively and be prepared to push it away with your camera, knife or tank. If a shark does bite a fellow diver, stop the bleeding, reassure the patient, treat for shock and seek immediate medical aid.

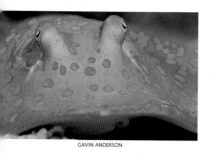
GAVIN ANDERSON

Stingray

Identified by its flattened, diamond-shaped body and wide "wings," the stingray has one or two venomous spines at the base of its tail. Stingrays like shallow water and tend to rest on silty or sandy bottoms, often burying themselves in the sand. Typically only the eyes, gill slits and tail are visible. These creatures are harmless unless you sit or step on them. Though injuries are uncommon, wounds are always extremely painful, and often deep and infective. Immerse wound in nonscalding hot water and seek medical aid.

Lionfish

Also known as turkeyfish or firefish, these slow, graceful fish extend their feathery pectoral fins as they swim. They have distinctive vertical brown or black bands alternating with narrower pink or white bands. When threatened or provoked, lionfish may inject venom through

GAVIN ANDERSON

dorsal spines that can penetrate booties, wetsuits and leather gloves. The wounds can be extremely painful. If stung, wash the wound and immerse in nonscalding hot water for 30 to 90 minutes.

Stonefish

Stonefish, as well as scorpionfish, inject venom through dorsal spines that can penetrate booties, wetsuits and gloves. They are often difficult to spot, since they typically rest quietly on the bottom or on coral, looking more like rocks. Practice good buoyancy control and watch where you put your feet and hands. Wounds can be excruciating. To treat a puncture, wash the wound and immerse in nonscalding hot water for 30 to 90 minutes.

GAVIN ANDERSON

Allergic victims who experience complications such as convulsions or cardiorespiratory failure should be transported to a hospital immediately.

Moray Eel

Distinguished by their long, thick, snake-like bodies and tapered heads, moray

GAVIN ANDERSON

eels come in a variety of colors and patterns. Don't feed them or put your hand in a dark hole—eels have the unfortunate combination of sharp teeth and poor eyesight and will bite if they feel threatened. If you are bitten, don't try to pull your hand away suddenly—the teeth slant backward and are extraordinarily sharp. Let the eel release your hand and then surface slowly. Treat with antiseptics, anti-tetanus and antibiotics.

Barracuda

Barracuda have long, silver, cylindrical bodies and razor-like teeth protruding from an underslung jaw. They swim alone or in small groups, continually opening and closing their mouths, an action that looks daunting but actually assists their respiration. Though barracuda will hover near divers to observe, they are really somewhat shy, though they may be attracted by shiny objects that resemble fishing lures. Irrigate a barracuda bite with fresh water and treat with antiseptics, antitetanus and antibiotics.

GAVIN ANDERSON

GAVIN ANDERSON

Titan Triggerfish

The largest of all triggerfish, this animal is usually no threat to divers, but it will aggressively defend its nest when guarding eggs. Best to give it a wide berth, as it has been known to attack divers for no apparent reason. If bitten, cleanse the wound thoroughly with soap, water and antiseptic, apply antibiotic ointment and monitor for signs of infection.

Sea Snake

Air-breathing reptiles with venom that's 20 times stronger than that of any land snake, sea snakes release venom only when feeding or under extreme distress—so most defensive bites do not contain venom. Sea snakes rarely bite even if they are handled, but avoid touching them. To treat a sea snake bite, use a pressure bandage and immobilize the victim. Try to identify the snake, be prepared to administer CPR, and seek urgent medical aid.

GAVIN ANDERSON

Fire Coral

Although often mistaken for stony coral, fire coral is a hydroid colony that secretes a hard, calcareous skeleton. Fire coral grows in many different shapes, often encrusting or taking the form of a variety of reef structures. It is usually identifiable by its tan, mustard or brown color and finger-like columns with

GAVIN ANDERSON

whitish tips. The entire colony is covered by tiny pores and fine, hair-like projections nearly invisible to the unaided eye. Fire coral "stings" by discharging small, specialized cells called nematocysts. Contact causes a burning sensation that lasts for several minutes and may produce red welts on the skin. Do not rub the area, as you will only spread the stinging particles. Cortisone cream can reduce the inflammation, and antihistamine cream is good for killing the pain. A doctor should treat serious stings.

Crown-of-Thorns

This large sea star may have up to 23 arms, although 13 to 18 are more commonly observed. Body coloration can be blue, green or grayish with the spines tinted red or orange. The spines are venomous and can deliver a painful sting even if the animal has been dead for two or three days. Also beware the toxic pedicellariae (pincers) between the spines, which can also cause severe pain upon contact. To treat stings, remove any loose spines, soak stung area in nonscalding hot water for 30 to 90 minutes and seek medical aid. Neglected wounds may produce serious injury. If you've been stung before, your reaction to another sting may be worse than the first.

EDWARD SNIJDERS

Sea Urchin

Sea urchins tend to live in shallow areas near shore and come out of their shelters at night. They vary in coloration and size, with spines ranging from short and

GAVIN ANDERSON

blunt to long and needle-sharp. The spines are the urchin's most dangerous weapon, easily able to penetrate neoprene wetsuits, booties and gloves. Treat minor punctures by extracting the spines and immersing in nonscalding hot water. More serious injuries require medical attention.

Jellyfish

Jellyfish sting by releasing the stinging cells contained in their trailing tentacles. As a rule, the longer the tentacles, the more painful the sting. Stings are often just irritating, not painful, but should be treated immediately with a decontaminant such as vinegar, rubbing alcohol, baking soda or dilute household ammonia. Be aware that some people may have a stronger reaction than others, in which case you should prepare to administer CPR and seek medical aid.

GAVIN ANDERSON

Diving Conservation & Awareness

EDWARD SNIJDERS

Increased diving and other human activities have placed immense pressure on the wonderful yet fragile marine ecosystem in the Red Sea. Marine preservation has become a major issue, especially in Egypt, where the stakes are the highest.

Sharm el-Sheikh and Hurghada, in particular, have suffered from uncontrolled building booms that have transformed their shorelines into resort strips attracting thousands of people a year—most of them divers. The environment has taken a hit from such development, as well as from the hundreds of dive boats that throng to local reefs every day. At the same time, tourism, notably dive tourism, is a major resource for Egypt and most of the region.

Accordingly, the last decade has seen a major shift in attitudes. The old days of dive boats dragging anchors across the reefs are gone, and several countries have set aside stretches of coastline as marine reserves, including the Coral Beach Nature Reserve in Israel, the Marine Peace Park in Jordan, and Egypt's world-renowned Ras Mohammed National Park.

Marine Reserves & Regulations

Egyptian authorities now control all coastal development and certify that it is environmentally sound. The Hurghada Environmental Protection & Conservation Association (see "Battle of the Buoys," opposite page) and the creation of Ras Mohammed National Park (see "Ras Mohammed Regulations," page 90) have been instrumental in building support for environmental protection.

HEPCA works closely with the Egyptian Environmental Affairs Agency (EEAA) to ensure that laws dealing with the protection of offshore islands and coral reefs are enforced. Its major achievement, though, has been to place some 500 mooring buoys and raise local environmental awareness. Marine rangers now police the seas, and boat captains found mooring to the reef rather than the buoys are prosecuted. This ambitious project is one of the biggest in the world in terms of diving conservation and has been successful thus far, though it needs more funding to be able to continue its work.

Environmental regulations advance a strict "look but don't touch" approach. Divers and snorkelers are prohibited from taking or molesting any form of marine life. Moreover, dive boats must tie to a mooring and can't drop anchor. Regulations are strictly enforced, and most dive operations and boat crews abide by the rules and are instrumental in enforcing them.

At reputable dive centers, the divemaster will address conservation matters during your pre-dive briefing. If your consoles drag on the bottom, expect to be politely but firmly alerted by the divemaster. Thankfully, most visitors are eco-friendly and adhere to the rules.

Battle of the Buoys

Conservationists estimate that more than 700 boats a week ply back and forth between Hurghada and the many reefs within an hour of town. By the late 1980s dive operators realized that you can't throw heavy steel anchors onto a reef day after day without a certain degree of damage. It sounds obvious now, but back then it was a bit of a revelation.

Local dive centers decided to take action. A makeshift solution was to chain mooring lines to the coral heads, but in 1992 HEPCA was founded, comprising some 15 dive operators. Their goal was to install permanent moorings. They chose the Manta Ray system, which features a permanent steel mooring held in place by wide flukes lodged beneath the sand, much like a buried anchor. Where the seabed is rock or coral, a hole is drilled and a huge pin cemented in. The system instantly reduced boat-related damage to the reefs.

Time took its toll on the buoys, however, and the dive centers had insufficient funds to properly maintain them. The U.S. Agency for International Development soon got involved, providing 250 additional buoys and training local captains on their proper use. Since then HEPCA has held a number of fund-raisers to pay for buoy upkeep, but problems persist.

During the first half of 2000, HEPCA covered 30 percent of the total mooring maintenance cost—the balance covered by the Egyptian Environmental Affairs Agency and the Red Sea Governorate. HEPCA's share consisted of membership fees and donations, as well as sales of the association's products. By July, however, HEPCA was obliged to stop the maintenance work due to a lack of funds—partly from the failure of some HEPCA members to pay dues. Until the situation is resolved, divers are urged to take particular care when visiting this already-stressed ecosystem.

JEAN-BERNARD CARILLET

Responsible Diving

Dive sites are often along reefs and walls covered in beautiful corals and sponges. It only takes a moment—an inadvertently placed hand or knee, or a careless brush or kick with a fin—to destroy this fragile, living part of our delicate ecosystem. By following certain basic guidelines while diving, you can help preserve the ecology and beauty of the reefs:

1. Never drop boat anchors onto a coral reef and take care not to ground boats on coral. Encourage dive operators and regulatory bodies in their efforts to establish permanent moorings at appropriate dive sites.

2. Practice and maintain proper buoyancy control and avoid overweighting. Be aware that buoyancy can change over the period of an extended trip. Initially you may breathe harder and need more weighting; a few days later you may breathe more easily and need less weight. Tip: Use your weight belt and tank position to maintain a horizontal position—raise them to elevate your feet, lower them to elevate your upper body. Also be careful about buoyancy loss: As you go deeper, your wetsuit compresses, as does the air in your BC.

3. Avoid touching living marine organisms with your body and equipment. Polyps can be damaged by even the gentlest contact. Never stand on or touch living coral. The use of gloves is no longer recommended: Gloves make it too easy to hold on to the reef. The abrasion caused by gloves may be even more damaging to the reef than your hands. If you must hold on to the reef, touch only exposed rock or dead coral.

4. Take great care in underwater caves. Spend as little time within them as possible, as your air bubbles can damage fragile organisms. Divers should take turns inspecting the interiors of small caves or under ledges to lessen the chances of damaging contact.

5. Be conscious of your fins. Even without contact, the surge from heavy fin strokes near the reef can do damage. Avoid full-leg kicks when diving close to the bottom and when leaving a photo scene. When you inadvertently kick something, stop kicking! It seems obvious, but some divers either panic or are totally oblivious when they bump something. When treading water in shallow reef areas, take care not to kick up clouds of sand. Settling sand can smother the delicate reef organisms.

6. Secure gauges, computer consoles and the octopus regulator so they're not dangling—they are like miniature wrecking balls to a reef.

7. When swimming in strong currents, be extra careful about leg kicks and handholds.

8. Photographers should take extra precautions, as cameras and equipment affect buoyancy. Changing f-stops, framing a subject and maintaining position for a photo often conspire to thwart the ideal "no-touch" approach on a reef. When you must use "holdfasts," choose them intelligently (i.e., use one finger only for leverage off an area of dead coral).

9. Resist the temptation to collect or buy coral or shells. Aside from the ecological damage, collection of marine souvenirs depletes the beauty of a site and spoils other divers' enjoyment.

10. Ensure that you take home all your trash and any litter you may find as well. Plastics in particular pose a serious threat to marine life.

11. Resist the temptation to feed fish. You may disturb their normal eating habits, encourage aggressive behavior or feed them food that is detrimental to their health.

12. Minimize your disturbance of marine animals. Don't ride on the backs of turtles or manta rays, as this can cause them great anxiety.

Marine Conservation Organizations

Coral reefs and oceans are facing unprecedented environmental pressures. The following groups are actively involved in promoting responsible diving practices, publicizing environmental marine threats and lobbying for better policies:

Local Organizations

Egypt

Hurghada Environmental Protection & Conservation Association (HEPCA)
☎/fax 065 445 035
www.hepca.org

National Parks of Egypt – Red Sea Protectorate
☎ 065 540 720 fax: 065 548 339

Sharm el-Sheikh Diving Union
☎/fax: 069 660 418
sharm_diving_union@sinainet.com.eg

Israel

The Society for the Protection of Nature in Israel
☎ 03 375 063 fax: 03-377 695
www.spni.org

Jordan

The Royal Society for the Conservation of Nature
relation@rscn.org.jo
www.rscn.org.jo

International Organizations

CEDAM International
☎ 914-271-5365
www.cedam.org

CORAL: The Coral Reef Alliance
☎ 510-848-0110
www.coral.org

Cousteau Society
☎ 757-523-9335
www.cousteausociety.org

Ocean Futures
☎ 805-899-8899
www.oceanfutures.com

Project AWARE Foundation
☎ 714-540-0251
www.projectaware.org

ReefKeeper International
☎ 305-358-4600
www.reefkeeper.org

Listings

Telephone Calls

To call Egypt, dial the international access code of the country you are calling from + 20 (Egypt's country code) + the area code without the 0 + the local number.

To call Israel, dial the international access code of the country you are calling from + 972 (Israel's country code) + the area code without the 0 + the local number.

To call Jordan, dial the international access code of the country you are calling from + 962 (Jordan's country code) + the area code without the 0 + the local number.

Diving Services

There are hundreds of dive centers throughout the Red Sea region, the majority in Egypt—at last count there were some 130 operators in Hurghada and 40 in Sharm el-Sheikh alone. There are far fewer reputable shops, however. Stick to well-established centers, where you'll find highly qualified instructors, top-notch facilities, environmental awareness and a wide range of diving services and products (see "Tips for Evaluating a Dive Operator," page 36).

The following is a broad (but not exhaustive) list of services available in the major regions covered in this guide, including telephone and fax numbers, as well as email and website addresses. Contact the dive shops directly for specific services.

Most dive centers are based on the grounds of big hotels, though all divers are welcomed and free pickup service is typically available. Most offer a range of rental gear and guided dives. Many offer certification and advanced diving classes and accept Open Water referrals. All facilities should display their appropriate affiliations (NAUI, PADI, SSI, CMAS, etc.). Major credit cards are widely accepted.

Psst ...Here's a Tip

As in a restaurant, a tip should reflect your level of satisfaction with the diving experience. If you're dissatisfied, tip less or not at all. But if the divemaster and boat crew went out of their way to make your dive safe and enjoyable, tip extra. Ten percent of the overall cost of the daytrip or live-aboard trip is generous. Tips are usually pooled among the crew, but an extra tip for a top-notch divemaster or instructor is acceptable.

Israel

Eilat

Aqua Sport International
☎ 07 633 4404 fax: 07 633 3771
info@aqua-sport.com
www.aqua-sport.com
Other: Aqua Sport Divers' Lodge in town
center; dive shop at Coral Beach

Dolphin Reef Eilat
☎ 07 637 5395 fax: 07 637 3824
reef@netvision.et.il
www.diversguide.com/dolphin_reef

Red Sea Sports Club
☎ 07 637 6569/0688 fax: 07 637 0655
manta1@netvision.net.il
www.redseasports.co.il
Other: Based at Ambassador Hotel on
Coral Beach

Jordan

Aqaba

Aquamarina Diving Center
☎ 03 201 6250–4 fax: 03 203 2630
aquama@go.com.jo
www.aquamarina-group.com/diving.html
Other: Based at Aquamarina I Beach
Club Hotel

The Royal Diving Centre
☎ 03 201 7035 fax: 03 201 7097
royaldiving@yahoo.com
Other: Just north of Saudi border

SeaStar Watersports
☎ 03 201 4131/2 fax: 03 201 4133
alcsea@alcazar.com.jo
www.seastar-watersports.com
Other: Based at Alcazar Hotel

Egypt

Nuweiba

Emperor Divers
☎ 069 520 320/1 fax: 069 520 327
info.nuweiba@emperordivers.com
www.emperordivers.com
Other: Based at Nuweiba Hilton
Coral Resort

Dahab

Divers International Dahab
☎/fax: 069 640 415
dahab@diversintl.com
www.diversintl.com
Other: Based at Ganet Sinai Resort

Fantasea Dive Club
☎ 062 640 483 ☎/fax: 062 640 043
fdc@intouch.com
www.divernet.com/fantasea

Egypt – Dahab (continued)

Inmo Dive Center
☎ 069 640 370/1 fax: 069 640 372
inmo@inmodivers.com
www.inmodivers.com
Other: Based at Inmo Divers Home hotel

Lagona Divers
☎ 069 640 356 fax: 069 640 355
dahab@lagona-divers.com
www.lagona-divers.com
Other: Based at Lagona Village hotel

Nesima Dive Center
☎ 069 640 320 fax: 069 640 321
nesima@intouch.com
www.nesima-resort.com
Other: Based at Nesima Resort

Reef 2000
☎/fax: 069 640 087
reef2000@intouch.com
www.reef2000.org
Other: Based at Bedouin Moon Hotel

Sinai Dive Club–Dahab
☎/fax: 069 640 465
sdclub@ritsec3.com.eg
www.geocities.com/TheTropics/2999/sdc.
html
Other: Based at Novotel

Sharm el-Sheikh

Anemone Dive Center
☎/fax: 069 600 999
anemone@sinainet.com.eg
Other: Based at Pigeon's House in
Na'ama Bay

Aquamarine Diving Centre
☎ 069 600 276 fax: 069 600 176
info@diversintl.com
www.diversintl.com
Other: Based at Novotel Coralia hotel in
Na'ama Bay

Camel Dive Club
☎ 069 600 700 fax: 069 600 601
reservations1@cameldive.com
www.cameldive.com
Other: Based at Camel Hotel in
Na'ama Bay

Colona Dive Club
☎ 069 662 222 fax: 069 602 624
colona@sinainet.com.eg
www.colona.com
Other: Based at Amar Sina Hotel on
Ras Umm Sid

**Divers International Sofitel
Diving Center**
☎ 069 603 130 fax: 069 600 176
info@diversintl.com
www.diversintl.com
Other: Based at Sofitel Hotel

Emperor Divers
☎ 069 601 734 fax: 069 601 735
info.sharm@emperordivers.com
www.emperordivers.com
Other: Based at Tropicana Rosetta Hotel
in Na'ama Bay

Ocean College Dive Centre
info@ocean-college.com
www.ocean-college.com
Other: Based at Ocean Lodge on Ras Umm
Sid (☎ 069 663 378 fax: 069 663 379)
and at Ocean Sands Hotel in Na'ama Bay
(☎ 069 600 802 fax: 069 600 950)

Oonas Dive Club
☎ 069 600 581/601 501 fax: 069 600 582
info@oonasdiveclub.com
www.oonasdiveclub.com
Other: Attached hotel; in Na'ama Bay

Egypt – Sharm el-Sheikh (continued)

Red Sea Diving College
☎ 069 600 145/245 fax: 069 600 144
info@sinai-services.com
www.redseadivingcollege.com
Other: Based in Na'ama Bay

Sinai Dive Club
www.dive-club.com
Other: Based at the Hilton Sharm
Dreams Resort (☎ 069 603 040;
diveclub.hd@dive-club.com), Hilton
Fayrouz Village (☎ 069 600 137–140;
diveclub.hf@dive-club.com) and Sonesta
Club (☎ 069 601 280; diveclub.sc@dive-
club.com) in Na'ama Bay

Sinai Divers
☎ 069 600 697 fax: 069 600 158
info@sinaidivers.com
www.sinaidivers.com
Other: Based at Ghazala Hotel in
Na'ama Bay

Subex
☎/fax: 069 601 388
sharm@subex.org
www.subex.org
Other: Based at Mövenpick Jolie Ville,
Baron Resort and Sharm Holiday Resort

El Gouna

The Dive Tribe
☎ 065 580 120 (ext. 8137)
fax: 065 545 160
info@divetribe.com
www.divetribe.com
Other: Based at Mövenpick Resort

Easy Divers
☎ 065 548 816 fax: 065 443 300
info@easydivers-redsea.com
www.easydivers-redsea.com
Other: Based at The Three Corners
Rihana hotel

TGI Marine Sporting Club
☎ 012 220 6427/224 2025
fax: 065 545 608
infogouna@tgidiving.com
www.tgidiving.com
Other: Based at Sheraton Miramar

Hurghada

Aquanaut Diving Center
☎ 065 549 891 fax: 065 547 045
info@aquanaut.net
www.aquanaut.net
Other: Based at Shedwan Golden
Beach Hotel

Blue Water Dive Resort
☎ 065 548 790/545 086 fax: 065 443
852/442 300
info@blue-water-dive.com
www.blue-water-dive.com
Other: Based at Arabia Beach Hotel and
Iberotel Arabella

Dive Point Red Sea
☎/fax: 065 442 019
hurghada@dive-point.com
www.dive-point.com
Other: Based at Coral Beach Hotel

Divers International Hurghada
☎ 065 549 747 (ext. 5505)
fax: 065 444 738
hurghada@diversintl.com
www.diversintl.com
Other: Based at Hilton Plaza

Egypt – Hurghada (continued)

Divers' Lodge Hurghada
☎ 065 446 911 fax: 065 446 910
tek@divers-lodge.com
www.divers-lodge.com
Other: Based at Intercontinental
Resort & Casino

Diving World Hurghada
☎ 010 530 3573 or 012 226 5636
dwhrg@hurghada.ie-eg.com
www.divingworldredsea.com
Other: Based at Sheraton Hotel

Easy Divers
☎ 065 548 816 fax: 065 443 300
info@easydivers-redsea.com
www.easydivers-redsea.com
Other: Based at The Three Corners
Village hotel

Emperor Divers
☎/fax: 065 444 854
info.hurghada@emperordivers.com
www.emperordivers.com
Other: Based at Hilton Resort

James & Mac Diving Center
☎ 012 311 8923 fax: 065 442 300
info@james-mac.com
www.james-mac.com
Other: Based at Giftun Beach Resort

Jasmin Diving Center
☎/fax: 065 446 455
info@jasmin-diving.com
www.jasmin-diving.com
Other: Based at Jasmine Village

**Red Sea for Tourism & Diving
(Rudi Kneip)**
☎ 065 442 960 fax: 065 442 234
info@rudi-direkt.com
www.rudi-direkt.com

Roland Schumm Dive Center
☎/fax: 065 442 422
rolandschummdiving@compuserve.com
www.hotelscape.com/roland

Sea Horse Diving Center
☎/fax: 065 547 621
seahorse@red-sea.com
www.red-sea.com/seahorse
Other: Based at Sea Horse Hotel

Sub Aqua Diving Center
☎/fax: 065 442 473
sofidive@hurghada.ie-eg.com
www.subaqua-diveteam.de
Other: Based at Sofitel Hotel

Subex
☎ 065 547 593 fax: 065 547 471
hurghada@subex.org
www.subex.org

Safaga

Barakuda Diving Center
☎/fax: 065 253 911
mahmoud@red-sea.com
www.red-sea.com/mahmoud
Other: Based at Lotus Bay Beach Resort

Duck's Dive Center
☎ 065 252 822–9 fax: 065 252 825
ddcredsea@t-online.de
www.red-sea.com/ducks
Other: Based at Holiday Inn; also based
in Quseir

Dune Diving Center
☎/fax: 065 253 075
info@duneredsea.com
www.duneredsea.com
Other: In front of police station

Easy Divers
☎ 065 548 816 fax: 065 443 300
info@easydivers-redsea.com
www.easydivers-redsea.com

Egypt – Safaga (continued)

Shams Safaga Diving Center
☎ 065 251 781–6 fax: 065 251 780
info@shamshotels.com
www.shamshotels.com
Other: Based at Shams Safaga Hotel

Sharm el-Naga Diving Center
☎/fax: 065 548 721
willysdive@red-sea.com
www.red-sea.com/sharmelnaga
Other: Based 40km (25 miles) south
of Hurghada

Quseir

Subex
☎ 065 332 100 fax: 065 332 124
elquseir@subex.org
www.subex.org
Other: Based at Mövenpick Resort on
Sirena Beach

Marsa Alam

Pioneer Divers
☎ 195 100 261 fax: 195 100 259
www.kahramana.com
Other: Based at Kahramana Blondie
Beach Resort

Red Sea Diving Safari
☎ 02 337 9942/1833 fax: 02 749 4219
redseasaf@hotmail.com
www.egypt.com/redsea
Other: Based at Marsa Shagra and
Marsa Nakari

Southern Red Sea

Diving in the southern Red Sea is done primarily via live-aboard. Political instability limits land-based dive travel opportunities. Eritrea is the least viable option right now, with Yemen not far behind. Prospects of diving in Sudan are the most promising, especially as the country enters the international oil markets.

Dive-Travel Specialists

Many companies specialize in arranging land-based and live-aboard dive trips. For the Red Sea it's best to book through an agent who has long-standing relationships with local operators. Following are some of the top dive-travel specialists in the U.K. and the U.S.:

United Kingdom

Aquatours
info@aquatours.com
www.aquatours.com

Goldenjoy Diving
sports@goldenjoy.co.uk
www.goldenjoy.co.uk

Diving World
surf@diving-world.com
www.diving-world.com

Hayes and Jarvis
diving@hayes-jarvis.com
www.hayes-jarvis.com

United Kingdom (continued)

Oonasdivers
info@oonasdivers.com
www.oonasdivers.com

Red Sea Divers
(live-aboards only)
david@redseadivers.com
www.redseadivers.com

Regal Diving
info@regal-diving.co.uk
www.regal-diving.co.uk

Tony Backhurst Scuba Centre
travel@scuba.co.uk
www.scuba.co.uk

United States

DiverPlanet
info@diverplanet.com
www.diverplanet.com

Island Dreams Travel
info@islandream.com
www.islandream.com

PADI Travel Network
ptn1@padi.com
www.padi.com

Reef and Rainforest
info@reefrainforest.com
www.reefrainfrst.com

Tropical Adventures
dive@divetropical.com
www.divetropical.com

World Dive Adventures
sales@worlddive.com
www.worlddive.com

Live-Aboards

Dozens of live-aboards ply the Red Sea, ranging from converted fishing boats to purpose-built luxury yachts, with itineraries ranging from two days to several weeks. Some may be booked directly, but most are best booked through dive-travel specialists. The following are some of the reputable live-aboards catering to an international clientele:

Diving World Fleet
Operates 10 live-aboards: *Miss Nouran, Royal Emperor, Mermaid, Greta, Sir Cousteau, Cyclone, Conquest I & II, Ishtar* and *Uscocco*
surf@diving-world.com
www.diving-world.com

Emperor Divers Fleet
Operates seven live-aboards: *Pegasus, Emperor 1, Emperor Mahy, El Waseem, Rosetta, LoveMan* and *Cairo 1*
reservations@emperordivers.com
www.emperordivers.com

Ghazala Fleet
Operates six live-aboards: *Ghazala Explorer, Ghazala Voyager, Ghazala Adventurer, Ghazala I & II* and *Lady M*
info@sinaidivers.com
www.sinaidivers.com

M/V *Oyster*
info@oysterdiving.com
www.oysterdiving.com

Red Sea Aggressor
info@aggressor.com
www.aggressor.com

Tourist Offices

Egypt's tourism ministry is on the web at http://touregypt.net. Israel's tourist office can be reached at www.infotour.co.il. Jordan's tourism board is at www.tourism.com.jo. Phone or visit the following local offices for more information, including brochures, maps and advice:

Egypt

Cairo
Airport (Terminals I and II)
☎ 02 667 475, ☎ 02 291 4255
5 Sharia Adly
☎ 02 391 3454

Hurghada
Sharia an-Nasr
☎ 065 446 513

Israel

Eilat
Yotam and Ha'Arava Roads
☎ 07 637 2111
Reservation & Information Center (open 24 hours)
Ha'Arava Road
☎ 07 637 4741/5944

Jordan

Aqaba
Prince Mohammed Street
☎ 03 201 4211

Index
dive sites covered in this book appear in **bold** type

Lonely Planet Pisces Books

The **Diving & Snorkeling** guides cover top destinations worldwide. Beautifully illustrated with full-color photos throughout, the series explores the best diving and snorkeling areas and prepares divers for what to expect when they get there. Each site is described in detail, with information on suggested ability levels, depth, visibility and, of course, marine life. There's basic topside information as well for each destination.

Also check out dive guides to:

Australia: Southeast Coast	Cozumel	Monterey Peninsula & Northern California	Seychelles
Baja California	Curaçao		Southern California
Belize	Dominica	Pacific Northwest	Texas
Bermuda	Florida Keys	Puerto Rico	Trinidad & Tobago
Bonaire	Guam & Yap	Roatan & Honduras' Bay Islands	Turks & Caicos
Cocos Island	Jamaica	Scotland	Vanuatu